Basic Training for the Supernatural Ways of Royalty

Basic Training for the Supernatural Ways of Royalty

Kris Vallotton

DESTINY IMAGE® PUBLISHERS, INC.

P.O. Box 310, Shippensburg, PA 17257-0310

"Speaking to the Purposes of God for this Generation and for the Generations to Come."

This book and all other Destiny Image, Revival Press, Mercy Place, Fresh Bread, Destiny Image Fiction, and Treasure House books are available at Christian bookstores and distributors worldwide.

For a U.S. bookstore nearest you, call **1-800-722-6774.**

For more information on foreign distributors, call **717-532-3040.**

Reach us on the Internet at **www.destinyimage.com.**

ISBN 10: 0-7684-2715-0

ISBN 13: 978-0-7684-2715-8

For Worldwide Distribution, Printed in the U.S.A.

2 3 4 5 6 7 8 9 10 11 / 12 11 10 09 08

ACKNOWLEDGMENTS

Allison and Carol—
thank you for all the hours that you poured into this book!

Contents

FOREWORD

ONE of the most amazing stories I have ever watched unfold has been the nearly 30-year-long journey of the author into a lifestyle of the supernatural. Kris and I have been friends for all that time, and partners in ministry for well over 20 years. His beginnings were the most humble imaginable. But there was a hunger and a willingness to serve that enabled him to rise both in experience and stature.

This journey began in Mountain Chapel of Weaverville, California. Day after day, Kris would look for any possible place to serve. His passion for more of an authentic gospel caused him to grow in maturity, and eventually to a place of leadership. He stood out because of his relentless pursuit of a supernatural lifestyle as a normal part of the everyday Christian experience. While he was born with strong prophetic gifting, it was not yet functioning in any practical sense in the early stages of his quest. But that soon changed. And many of the breakthroughs we experienced in those years were in part due to Kris's gift.

After moving to Redding, California, to pastor Bethel Church, I asked Kris to come and join my staff. He said yes and left the business world to do so. That was about nine years ago. Some go to seminary or Bible college to get trained. But Kris went into the marketplace to do his learning, as it was God's assignment for that season of his life. It would be in that environment that God would train Kris in the things he had hoped to learn in a school: the normal Christian life of miracles, signs, and wonders. After joining our staff, God added to Kris's schooling by exposing him to another world—church life. It was the combination of the two that God used to give him an extraordinary wisdom about the supernatural lifestyle both in and out of the church. What he teaches, he lives.

Kris's journey continues, as does mine. There is more available to all who will give themselves completely to displaying an authentic gospel. My heart is that you would give yourself to honoring our Lord Jesus Christ by displaying His love, character, and power. This book will go a long way in making the much-desired supernatural lifestyle a reality in your life. I highly recommend both the man and message; for they are one and the same.

Bill Johnson, Senior Pastor
Bethel Church
Redding, California

INTRODUCTION

E are called to be sons and daughters of the King, a royal priesthood and a people of prominence. But so many of us have no idea how royalty behaves. We often can't comprehend the difference between the noble and the common.

I was raised in a very poor family, and I had never been to a restaurant until a girl asked me to a Sadie Hawkins dance in high school. The young lady was going to take me out to a nice steakhouse and then we would go to the dance. The night before the big date, my mom spent the evening showing me how to conduct myself in a restaurant. She sat me down at a table with a full set of silverware. She taught me to put the napkin on my lap before I ate. She exhorted me several times to keep my elbows off the table and chew with my mouth closed. She instructed me in which piece of silverware I was to use first. She reminded me to pull the chair out and seat my date before I sat down. I just had no idea how ignorant I was until my mother gave me that lesson in etiquette.

This is a great example of the way so many of us grew up in the Kingdom. We were adopted into the King's family, but we just don't have a clue about how to act in the palace. Many people who read *The Supernatural Natural Ways of Royalty* have been asking me for some more practical training on how to apply those truths to their lives. We wrote this workbook for those who have read the book and captured many of the principles but still needed a deeper path to see the nature of God assimilated into their lives more completely. This workbook should help you to dispel the pauper mindset and integrate royalty into the deepest core of who you are.

The workbook is arranged to assist you as you unearth the treasures that lie inside of you and discover the lies that are constraining you. As you read on, you will find yourself on a Holy Spirit journey into the very heart of God. I encourage you to stop often to consider what is really being asked of you or stated in the text. This workbook is meant to be a comprehensive, soul-searching experience that will hopefully be a catalyst to a contemplative season of transformation.

Let the journey begin!

Chapter 1

THE PLIGHT OF PAUPERHOOD

...I went to bed, fell asleep, and had a dream. In the dream a voice kept repeating this Scripture: "*Under three things the earth quakes, and under four, it cannot bear up: under a pauper when he becomes king*" (Prov. 30:21-22a) (Vallotton, 2006, 21).[1]

 *HE Supernatural Ways of Royalty* flows from the implications of this verse. On the one hand, it is fairly easy to understand what this verse is talking about, even though we don't really have kings in our society. Our "rags to riches" stories usually involve someone who wins the lottery or gets a big break in the film or music industry. And we know enough of these stories to understand that hitting the jackpot doesn't always make life rosy. On the other hand, it's easy to miss the fact that this verse really applies to all of us, not just lottery winners. What the Lord wants us to realize is that, at our conversion, we hit the jackpot. We went from rags to riches. We just don't really know it or understand how to handle it yet, and this is causing problems.

We need to learn a couple of things. First, we need to understand why things fall apart when paupers rule. Second, we need to learn how to leave the rags behind us for good and learn to be kings so we can handle the riches. The earth can only bear up when a true king rules.

Let's begin by unpacking the following explanation for the verse:

A pauper is born into insignificance. As he grows up he learns through life that he has no value and his opinions don't really matter. Therefore, when he becomes a king, he is important to the world around him but he still feels insignificant in the world that lies within him. Subsequently, he doesn't watch his words or the way he carries himself. He ultimately destroys the very people that he is called to lead (Vallotton, 22).

WHAT IS A PAUPER?

The Oxford American Dictionary defines a *pauper* as "a very poor person," and it defines *poor* as "lacking sufficient money to live at a standard considered comfortable or normal in a society" or simply "deficient or lacking." *A **pauper** is defined by **lack.*** And certainly, lack can exist not just in the area of money but in every area of human need including food, shelter, safety, education, affection, relationship, peace, and joy. Thus, *paupers of different kinds exist at every economic level of society.*

    ✒ Take some time to consider and write down some areas of your life where you have experienced lack.

    _____

    _____

    _____

    ✒ The dictionary defines *insignificance* as "lacking power or influence." How has the lack in your life contributed to feelings or thoughts of powerlessness in your life?

    _____

    _____

    _____

THE WORLD WITHIN

As he grows up he learns through life that he has no value and his opinions don't really matter. Therefore, when he becomes a king, he is important to the world around him but he still feels insignificant in the world that lies within him (Vallotton, 22).

What is the world that lies within a person? It is the set of core beliefs and assumptions that we use to interpret the world around us. The tricky thing about this set of beliefs is that we develop it largely unconsciously. Every day as we experience life we are drawing conclusions about the way the world works, about who we are, about who other people are, and about the meaning of life.

One way to help see "the world within" us is to ask ourselves what we learned to be true in childhood. Take some time and write down the "Ten Commandments" that defined your household as a child. These might be rules or statements of belief about the nature and purpose of life, such as "God helps those who help themselves."

1. _____

2. _____

3. _____

4. _____

5. _____

6. _____

7. _____

8. _____

9. _____

10. _____

☙ Now take a look at your list. Since you've become a Christian, have you discovered that any of these rules or beliefs aren't in line with what God says is true? How are these wrong beliefs affecting your life?

_____

_____

_____

LIVING AS ELEPHANTS

You may have heard the story about a man who observed an adult elephant that was tied by a rope to a stake in the ground. He saw that the elephant could easily break free of this constraint, so he asked the elephant keeper why it stayed put. The keeper explained that if you tie an elephant up when it's little and it can't break free, it will still believe that the rope is stronger than it even after it gets big.

Paupers who become kings are like that elephant. They've been tied up all their lives by lack, and even when the lack is gone, they still think like they did when they lacked. Lack, and its message of insignificance, creates a prison in our minds.

We leave the prison of sin and poverty through accepting what Christ did for us on the Cross, but we don't leave the prison in our minds right away because our understanding of what this event means is limited at first. Most of us think it's about us receiving forgiveness for our individual sins. But it's far more than that, and unless we step more fully into what really happened at our conversion, we will be living in a dream world. What does living in a dream world look like? Consider the following statement:

> I was not raised with the idea that I was significant. This caused me to develop a whole set of behaviors that someone like Moses would probably have never displayed. Even after I got saved, many of these behaviors stayed around. I saw that Nancy's confrontation was about more than her simply being sensitive and me being misunderstood, which was the way I wanted to interpret it. It was about me doing things that I've always done, but which are no longer consistent with who God says that I am (Vallotton, 23).

What kinds of habits in your life have you had to leave behind in order to act more consistently with whom God says you are? What habits can you see in your life that still need to change?

_____

_____

_____

WAKING UP

When he becomes a king, he is important to the world around him (Vallotton, 22).

Did you know that you have become important to the world around you? Take a look at how the apostle Peter describes who you are:

But you are a chosen generation, a royal priesthood, a holy nation, His own special people, that you may proclaim the praises of Him who called you out of darkness into His marvelous light...having your conduct honorable among the Gentiles, that when they speak against you as evildoers, they may, by your good works which they observe, glorify God in the day of visitation (1 Peter 2:9,12).

Think about what it means to be each of the following things and write down some thoughts about how someone who is characterized by them would think and act:

Chosen:

_____

_____

_____

Royal:

_____

_____

_____

Holy:

_____

_____

_____

Special:

_____

_____

_____

Honorable:

_____

_____

_____

CARRYING OURSELVES

What three words would you choose to describe your identity as a Christian?

_____

_____

_____

🕮 Now, based on your description, what are three kinds of behavior that you exhibit as expressions of those three words?

_____

_____

_____

🕮 What three words would you choose to describe the role of a Christian?

_____

_____

_____

🕮 Name three responsibilities that Christians have as a result of their role.

_____

_____

_____

🕮 Imagine that you had been appointed as president of the United States, but didn't understand the responsibilities of that role. What are some of the things that could happen?

_____

_____

_____

Consider the following exhortation that Paul gave to the Ephesians:

I, therefore, the prisoner of the Lord, beseech you to walk worthy of the calling with which you were called (Ephesians 4:1).

What happens when the way we are walking is not worthy of the calling to which we have been called? What happens when we have a role of significance and a mindset of insignificance? What happens when we are important to the world but don't know it?

_____

_____

_____

Subsequently, he doesn't watch his words or the way he carries himself. He ultimately destroys the very people that he is called to lead (Vallotton, 22).

Most of us have experienced what it's like to be on the receiving end of a Christian who is not aware of how his or her words or behavior are negatively affecting us. Based on that experience, what would you say that it costs the people around you when you are careless about the way you carry yourself?

_____

_____

_____

CONCLUSION

The way we perceive ourselves and our world determines how we behave. But it's possible for us to have a self-perception and a perspective on the world that is largely out of line with the truth, even if we have embraced the truth that we are forgiven of sin through faith in Christ. There is a larger truth than the fact that we are forgiven. That truth is that we have been made sons and daughters of God, the King of the universe. As sons and daughters, we have a calling that we must learn to walk worthy of, a calling far greater than any of us have ever imagined.

As a closing exercise, imagine your day so far—what you've done, where you've been, and what you've said. Now imagine how your day might be different if you really believed your Dad was the King of the universe. What would you say and do?

_____

_____

_____

_____

_____

_____

_____

_____

ENDNOTE

1. Interestingly, this version of this verse with the term "pauper" does not appear in any of the common Bible translations, but it was how the verse was stated in the dream.

Chapter 2

CASTLE TRAMPS OR PALACE PRINCES

When Nancy confronted me about the damage my humor was doing, I realized that it wasn't just a wake-up call to the fact that I was hurting people. The greater revelation, to me, was that people valued what I had to say. I had always believed what my stepfathers had drilled into me: people didn't really care what I thought or said. *The realization that I had value began the process of uprooting the lies I believed about myself and helped me find out who I actually was.* God had called me a prince, and I realized that that meeting with Nancy and the interaction I had with the Lord would just be the first of many steps that God would use to lead me out of my prison and into His palace. (Vallotton, 27-28)

☙ Describe what you know about the circumstances surrounding your birth. Did you receive the message from your parents that you had value?

_____

_____

_____

☙ Do you feel like people value what you have to say? Do you feel like God values what you have to say?

_____

_____

_____

☙ With whom do you feel the most loved and accepted for who you are? How does that person or group of people communicate a message of love and acceptance to you?

_____

_____

_____

☙ Scripture tells us that God is love, but knowing *that* God loves us, and experiencing His love *for* us are two different things. Describe a time when you experienced the personal love and acceptance of God. How did this experience change the way you felt and thought about yourself?

_____

_____

_____

SABOTAGING OUR RELATIONSHIPS

The writer of the verse in Proverbs about paupers becoming princes, goes on to list three more things under which "the earth quakes" and "cannot bear up," (see Prov. 30:21-22) including the following:

...an unloved woman when she gets a husband... (Proverbs 30:23 NASB).

That word *unloved* (NASB) is also translated "hateful" (NKJV) or "bitter" (NLT). Lack of love in your life trains you to believe that you are unlovable, and that self-hatred and bitterness create a brokenness that renders you unable to receive and contain the love of another person.

The spouse or friend who tries to love you finds that the hope of having a safe, intimate relationship with you is severely threatened by the scars that the poverty of love in your life has created.

❦ Have you ever tried to love someone who doesn't love himself or herself? How did that person respond to your expressions of love or kindness? How did his or her response make you feel?

_____

_____

_____

Whenever someone values us more than we value ourselves we tend to sabotage our relationship with that person. Secretly, we don't want them to get close enough to find out that we aren't as good as they think we are. (Vallotton, 30)

❦ Have you been in a relationship that was sabotaged by the other person in that relationship? Have you every sabotaged a relationship? In either case, do you feel like you understand what happened and why? Were insecurity and self-hatred influencing your behavior or the behavior of the other person?

_____

_____

_____

_____

_____

_____

One of the most common ways that we sabotage relationships is through *neglect*. Healthy relationships require intentional and regular displays of love—serving each other, showing vulnerability, being together, and so forth. But if we are insecure and a relationship exposes our insecurity, it's a knee-jerk reaction for many of us to withdraw physically, mentally, or emotionally from the other person.

> ❧ Have you ever gotten close to someone and then felt like the relationship had gotten too close for comfort? Do you think this discomfort was related to your insecurity? What did you do and why?

_____

_____

_____

LEARN TO LOVE YOURSELF

If you struggle with insecurity and self-hatred and find it hard to build intimacy and trust in relationships, the Lord's answer is as true for you as it was for Kris: "Learn to love yourself as much as I love you." Consider the following scriptures:

Make yourselves at home in my love (John 15:9 The Message).

In this is love, not that we loved God, but that He loved us and sent His Son to be the propitiation for our sins. Beloved, if God so loved us, we also ought to love one another. No one has seen God at any time. If we love one another, God abides in us, and His love has been perfected in us (1 John 4:10-12).

And we have known and believed the love that God has for us. God is love, and he who abides in love abides in God, and God in him (1 John 4:16).

There is no fear in love; but perfect love casts out fear, because fear involves torment. But he who fears has not been made perfect in love. We love Him because He first loved us (1 John 4:18-19).

God's perfect love is the supreme antidote to all of our fear and insecurity, and *experiencing* the reality of God's love for us is what gives us the capacity to love God, ourselves, and others. If we are going to love ourselves as much as God loves us, then we must encounter His love for us. This is why the apostle Paul prayed the following prayer for you and all other believers:

I bow my knees to the Father of our Lord Jesus Christ, from whom the whole family in Heaven and earth is named, that He would grant you, according to the riches of His glory, to be strengthened with might through His Spirit in the inner man, that Christ may dwell in your hearts through faith; that you, being rooted and grounded in love, may be able to comprehend with all the saints what is the width and length and depth and height—to know the love of Christ which passes knowledge; that you may be filled with all the fullness of God (Ephesians 3:14-19).

Did you catch the fact that it takes *might* (Greek: *dunamis*) to comprehend and know the love of God that passes knowledge? God's love is so awesome that we can't even begin to get it without receiving a transfer of supernatural power.

Who is the Person who is going to give us this power? It's the Holy Spirit.

❧ Take some time and talk to the Holy Spirit and ask Him to give you His power to know His love. As you pray, remember the promise that the apostle John, who had one of the greatest revelations of the love of God in the Bible, recorded in his Gospel and his letters:

Now this is the confidence that we have in Him, that if we ask anything according to His will, He hears us. And if we know that He hears us, whatever we ask, we know that we have the petitions that we have asked of Him (1 John 5:14-15).

STARTING OVER

Eddie was always afraid he would not have enough...But the fear of lack is based on lies, and until those lies are broken, people can't recognize God's provision for their lives. When Eddie became part of our family he had everything he needed and wanted. His old life was gone. But until he stopped believing those lies he couldn't relax and enjoy life with us (Vallotton, 34).

Eddie is a great example of how we all behave when we come into the Kingdom. Our behavior reveals that we really don't understand what has happened to us, and that we're unaware of the fact that we don't understand. This is perhaps the primary reason that Jesus made the following statements about our entrance into the Kingdom:

Assuredly, I say to you, whoever does not receive the kingdom of God as a little child will by no means enter it (Mark 10:15).

Most assuredly, I say to you, unless one is born again, he cannot see the kingdom of God (John 3:3).

Jesus describes our conversion as a *birth*, and says we must become like *children*. The message is: "You have to start over." Our conversion is, once again, not merely about being forgiven; it's about learning how to do life all over again, and to do it differently this time. But unlike children, most of us feel like we already know some things about ourselves and the world when we come to Christ. The challenge for us is that the journey of knowing, trusting and becoming sure of God means admitting that actually we *don't* know, that we *can't* trust the things we used to, and we *can't* be sure that what we've always thought was real actually is real. This is why receiving a childlike, teachable, humble spirit is so important.

It is this spirit that helps us give up the lies we have believed and learn the truth, particularly about the provision of God. Everything we could ever need or desire is available to us in the Kingdom of God. But like Eddie, we won't see it until we believe it.

What are some things that you used to believe about yourself and the world that you discovered were completely untrue when you came to Christ? How comfortable are you with the idea that you probably have some similar discoveries to make ahead of you? Which would you say is more important to you—being right, or being sure that God loves you?

_____

_____

_____

_____

SONS, NOT SERVANTS

Why in the world did the older brother hang out waiting for his father to give him a goat when he owned the whole farm? He failed to recognize that he was a son and not a servant. *The revelation of our true identity will destroy the spirit of poverty in our lives.* But until that happens we will keep thinking that there are limits on what we get to have. As a result, we are jealous of anyone who receives something that we don't have. This leaks into all aspects of our lives, including work, friends, and positions within the church (Vallotton, 35).

☙ When you came to Christ, did you learn that being "born again" meant that you were actually born into an entirely new relationship to God—that you were now His son or daughter? Would you say that being God's daughter or son is primarily how you think of yourself in relationship to God?

_____

_____

_____

_____

☙ Most of us know what it feels like to look at someone else's life, see what we don't have and feel like we're missing out. Think of an example of when this has happened in your life and describe 1) what you saw that you wanted and 2) what you did about this longing.

_____

_____

_____

_____

ASK, SEEK, KNOCK

Did you know that one of the primary ways we demonstrate our relationship as sons and daughters of our Father is by asking Him for things? Jesus put it this way:

> *Ask, and it will be given to you; seek, and you will find; knock, and it will be opened to you. For everyone who asks receives, and he who seeks finds, and to him who knocks it will be opened. Or what man is there among you who, if his son asks for bread, will give him a stone? Or if he asks for a fish, will he give him a serpent? If you then, being evil, know how to give good gifts to your children, how much more will your Father who is in heaven give good things to those who ask Him!* (Matthew 7:7-11)

❧ Maybe one of the reasons the older brother in the story of the prodigal son never got that goat that he wanted was that he never asked for it! Do you regularly come to the Father with your needs and desires? Why or why not?

_____

_____

_____

_____

❧ Think about the verse from First John you read earlier (see 1 John 5:14-15). Do you feel *confident* that when you pray, God hears you and answers you? Why or why not?

_____

_____

_____

_____

Owning Things

When a pauper gets a lot of money, the question that needs to be answered is, "Did God gain a fortune or lose a man?" Paupers often lose sight of their priorities when they get money, but *princes don't get their identity from what they have because they know their identity is not dependent on their performance or their possessions.* Princes own things, but they never let things own them. The result is that they are able to experience the worry-free life Jesus promised and are free to seek first the kingdom, knowing that all they need will be added to them (Vallotton, 37).

"Princes own things." In fact, the apostle Paul tells us that we, the sons and daughters of God, have inherited "all things" (see 1 Cor. 3:21). The doctrine that poverty in itself is a virtue is not from God. In fact, poverty is one of the primary expressions of the kingdom of sin and death. Poverty of all kinds is terribly destructive, and clearly reflects the work of the devil, who comes to steal, kill, and destroy (see John 10:10). Our God is a rich God, and He's a generous God. So when Jesus told the rich young ruler to sell all he had and give it to the poor, for example, He wasn't pointing out that poverty is a good thing (see Luke 18:22). He was pointing out that sometimes we get into a wrong relationship with the good things that God gives us and start trusting in them more than the One who gave them. And sometimes the primary thing that exposes this wrong relationship is the threat of losing that which we are trusting.

&- Is there anything in your life that you would not be willing to give to God, if He asked for it?

_____

_____

_____

_____

_____

_____

GOD'S FULL PROVISION

Abraham is probably one of the greatest examples of someone who withheld nothing from God, even his most precious possession. When he offered Isaac to God on Mount Moriah, he received one of the greatest revelations of God's nature in the Bible, the revelation of God's provision:

> *And Abraham called the name of the place, The-Lord-Will-Provide; as it is said to this day, "In the Mount of the Lord it shall be provided"* (Genesis 22:14).

As a result, the Lord gave Abraham one of the greatest promises in the Bible:

> *By Myself I have sworn, says the Lord, because you have done this thing, and have not withheld your son, **your only son**—blessing I will bless you, and multiplying I will multiply your descendants as the stars of the heaven and as the sand which is on the seashore; and your descendants shall possess the gate of their enemies. In your seed all the nations of the earth shall be blessed, because you have obeyed My voice* (Genesis 22:16-18).

Funny enough, Isaac wasn't Abraham's only son. But he was the son of promise, and when Abraham gave him to God something powerful happened, because it just so happened that God was planning to give His only Son, not only to Abraham's descendants, but to the human race. Abraham experienced a measure of God's provision when he gave his son to God, but when God gave us His Son, He released the *full provision* of Heaven onto the earth. Jesus made all the resources of Heaven available to all who would step into sonship with His Father through faith in Him. The more we understand what the Cross accomplished, the more the issue of God's provision in our lives should be fully settled in our hearts. Fear of lack is completely foreign to the mind of a son and daughter of God. The apostle Paul put it this way:

> *He who did not spare His own Son, but delivered Him up for us all, how shall He not with Him also freely give us all things?* (Romans 8:32)

CONCLUSION

The Holy Spirit has been assigned to believers to lead us into all truth, particularly the truth of God's love for us and our identity as His sons and daughters. You've already spent some time asking Him to empower you to know His love more fully. Now spend some time asking Him to help you to comprehend the reality that in Christ *all things are yours*.

Chapter 3

DUNGEONS AND DRAGONS

Jesus said, "You will know the truth, and the truth will set you free" (John 8:32 NIV). The word *truth* here means "reality." So many of us live in a "virtual reality"; it feels real and looks real, but it isn't real (Vallotton, 48).

HE reason things fall apart when a pauper becomes a king is that he is living in a virtual reality, conforming to old patterns of thinking and behavior that directly contradict his new identity and position. The fact that we can believe something to be true and experience it as true when it's not really true points to the power of belief.

Some people use the power of belief as an argument for relativism, claiming that truth is entirely a subjective matter. Christianity proposes a different explanation: that there is *truth*, which is *God's version of reality*; and lies, which are *distortions of the truth* promoted by the father of lies, the devil. The fact that lies can feel real comes from the fact that reality flows from the spiritual realm to the natural realm, and it flows through the gate, if you will, of human belief, trust, and agreement. When we trust in lies, we are actually giving permission for the enemy to release his destructive power in our lives to make those lies our reality. But when we trust in the truth, we align ourselves with the reality of the kingdom of God, and it manifests in our lives.

So how exactly do you "trust" or "agree with" either truth or lies? I'm glad you asked.

REFLECTION, MEDITATION, AND IMAGINATION

The watering hole is a place of *reflection*, which means both gazing at something and meditating on it. Meditation involves our imagination. If we feed our imagination with thoughts of what we don't want to become and drink from the well of regret, we reproduce that very thing in ourselves. It doesn't matter *what we want to reproduce.* It's only important *what we imagine* while we are thinking and drinking at the watering hole of our imagination (Vallotton, 41).

The first principle of belief to consider is this: *that which you focus on will determine your reality.* Every day, all day long, our minds are receiving information from the world around us and interpreting our experiences. Our minds filter out that which we have learned to be irrelevant and enable us to focus in on what is most important. But that which is important to us is connected to something else. Consider the following verse:

And God saw that the wickedness of man was great in the earth, and that every **imagination of the thoughts of his heart was only evil continually** (Genesis 6:5 KJV).

This verse makes a connection between our *imaginations*, our *thoughts*, and our *hearts*. That which fills our daydreams and our thoughts—that which is important to us—is connected to the heart, which is the seat of our emotions and desires. Proverbs states:

Keep your heart with all diligence, for out of it spring the issues of life (Proverbs 4:23).

This explains why whatever we focus on will become our reality, for that which captures our attention, focus, and imagination will fill our hearts. *That which fills our hearts is that which will fill our lives, for life flows from the heart.*

&- Think through the last few days and remember a time that you spent focusing on, imagining, or reflecting on something. What was it and what was your emotional state during that time? Was it something you think about a lot? If so, how does it connect to a significant desire or value in your life?

_____

_____

_____

BE ANXIOUS FOR NOTHING

Let's consider a specific area where we can see that our focus creates a certain reality in our lives. Some of the primary things that grab our attention and lock us into an intense focus are *problems*. When there's a problem, whether it's a question that needs to be answered or an obstacle to be overcome, it's amazing how it can take over your world. Solving problems feels great, but the thing about problems when we're in the middle of them is that, more often than not, we start to believe a lie about reality, which opens the door to anxiety and fear in our lives.

Worry, anxiety, and fear are so commonplace in our society that it's hard for many of us to imagine life without it. Most of the time we simply call it "stress." But did you know that the roots of the words *worry* and *anxious* actually both mean "to strangle" or "choke"?[1] This reveals the true nature of fear, anxiety, and stress—the reality that these things create in our lives is destructive to our bodies, minds and emotions.

   Describe a time when you experienced or saw the power of anxiety in your life or the life of someone you know. How did it affect you or the person you know physically? Mentally? Emotionally?

_____

_____

_____

Both Jesus and the apostle Paul instructed us never to worry or be anxious, because at best we are agreeing with lies when we do so. The apostle Paul also gave us a doctor's prescription for how to guard our hearts against anxiety in the midst of problems. He said:

> *Be anxious for nothing, but in everything by prayer and supplication, with thanksgiving, let your requests be made known to God; and the peace of God, which surpasses all understanding, will guard your hearts and minds through Christ Jesus. Finally, brethren, whatever things are true, whatever things are noble, whatever things are just, whatever things are pure, whatever things are lovely, whatever things are of good report, if there is any virtue and if there is anything praiseworthy—meditate on these things* (Philippians 4:6-8).

❧ The first thing that Paul tells us to do is to give our requests to God. Why do you suppose it's important that thanksgiving be an ingredient in our requests?

_____

_____

_____

_____

_____

_____

❧ Notice that Paul's first statement is an "if, then" statement. If we give our requests to God, *then* He will set up a protective wall of peace around our hearts and minds. So you know that you've been successful in giving God the problem or the need when you start to experience His peace! Describe a time when you felt the peace that passes understanding. Did this experience coincide with a change in your perspective towards your circumstances?

_____

_____

_____

_____

_____

_____

The last thing that Paul tells us to do connects with the principle that we've been considering. After we've given God our requests (and often, repented from a wrong focus on our circumstances that has led to an agreement with fear), we must start filling our minds with the right things so that we can build an agreement with the reality of the Kingdom. Spend some time listing some things that meet the following criteria:

Just:

_____

_____

_____

_____

Pure:

_____

_____

_____

_____

Lovely:

_____

_____

_____

Of Good Report:

_____

_____

_____

_____

Virtuous:

_____

_____

_____

_____

Praiseworthy:

_____

_____

_____

_____

RESPONDING TO THE CALL OF GOD

What I am realizing about many of us is that we spend much of our lives react-ing to what we don't want to be instead of responding to the call of God on our lives. We waste a lot of energy trying not to be something. In order to not be something I have to keep it in front of me so I can avoid it. The crazy thing is that I reproduce what I imagine. If I see what I don't want to be, just envisioning it causes me to reproduce it....We break out of this prison by responding to the call of God on our lives and meditating on His vision for us (Vallotton, 41-42).

❧ Have you found yourself behaving in ways that you specifically were trying to avoid, or even swore you would never do? If so, how were your choices connected to a mindset of reacting to what you don't want to be instead of responding to God?

_____

_____

_____

_____

❧ We define ourselves, our calling and our world *positively* when we focus on who we are, what is going on around us and what God is doing in our lives. We define them *negatively* when we focus on who we are not, what's not happening, and what it seems that God is not doing. Would you say that you are a person who primarily hangs out in the realm of negative definition or the realm of positive definition? How is that working out for you?

_____

_____

_____

_____

❧ Spend a few moments writing down some of the primary aspects of who God has called you to be. How much time do you spend meditating on who God has called you to be?

_____

_____

_____

_____

_____

_____

_____

_____

_____

_____

_____

_____

_____

_____

BITTERNESS AND JEALOUSY

Unforgiveness causes us to waste our lives trying to get even instead of fulfilling our own destiny by walking in our call. It is important that we forgive all those who sinned against us so that we can be free to go on with our lives. It is also crucial that we learn to forgive ourselves for our own sins (Vallotton, 42).

Clearly, some of the biggest problems that arrest our focus are the mistakes we all make. As the parable on forgiveness in Matthew 18 implies, the issue of forgiving others and ourselves becomes clear in the context of what it means to be forgiven, which we will look at in the next chapter (see Vallotton 43-44). The point here is that as long as our focus is locked on what we or other people have done or not done, our focus cannot be locked on what we are called to do and what God is doing. Forgiveness is a vital step in *repenting* for our wrong focus.

The lie we believe when we fixate on that which other people have done or not done to us, as well as that which we have done or not done, is that those things are a greater reality than the reality of that which God has done and will do for us. Forgiving others and ourselves helps to break our agreement with that lie. Significantly, this is almost the same lie that we believe when we allow jealousy to enter our hearts. We think what someone else has is a greater reality than what God has for us. Believing these lies brings us into agreement with the spirits of bitterness and jealousy, allowing them to bring their destruction into our lives.

 Have you ever felt like you could never get over something you had done or someone had done to you? Or, have you ever felt that someone else's success or possessions robbed or diminished you in some way? Describe one such situation and write down how these beliefs affected your behavior and emotions.

_____

_____

_____

_____

THE REAL BATTLE

Paul told us that transformation in our lives is directly the result of our minds being renewed (see Rom. 12:2). Our behavior only really changes when we change the way we think and believe. This is why this realm of faith, trust, belief, and agreement with either the truth or lies is where the real battle of our lives is situated. Paul also said:

For though we walk in the flesh, we do not war according to the flesh. For the weapons of our warfare are not carnal but mighty in God for pulling down strong-holds, casting down arguments and every high thing that exalts itself against the knowledge of God, bringing every thought into captivity to the obedience of Christ (2 Corinthians 10:4-5).

What are the weapons of warfare? What has the power to break the power of lies in our lives? It is the truth. The truths of the Kingdom are the weapons that destroy lies and transform our minds and lives, because they not only expose the inferior, false reality of lies, but also draw us into the superior reality of the Kingdom.

❧ Consider the situation you described in the last question, or another situation that you or someone you know may be facing in which issues of bitterness, jealousy, or anxiety are involved. Spend some time asking the Holy Spirit to reveal the superior truths by which these lies can be cast down. Write down what you hear.

_____

_____

_____

_____

_____

CONFESSING WITH OUR MOUTHS

We see the weapons of truth at work in the stories in this chapter of the women who were delivered from demonic torment—one through forgiveness and one through renouncing a lie she had believed (Vallotton, 45-46, 49). In both cases the Holy Spirit revealed the truth of their situation, and this truth exposed strongholds in their lives and gave them the opportunity to pull those strongholds down. But there was another element in these stories that we must consider. Both of them had to *say something* to step into their freedom. Similarly, as Paul taught us, we need to *give our requests* to God in order to step into agreement with His peace that passes understanding. This has to do with a second principle of belief, and that is that *our words work with the thoughts of our heart in creating trust and agreement with either the truth or lies.* We see this principle expressed by Paul in Romans 10:9:

*If you **confess with your mouth** the Lord Jesus and **believe in your heart** that God has raised Him from the dead, you will be saved* (Romans 10:9).

CONCLUSION

Taking the truth the Holy Spirit has unveiled to you about the situations you've been considering in the last two questions, spend some time making a transaction with Him. Give Him your requests, with thanksgiving. Verbally forgive anyone you need to forgive, including yourself. Renounce any lies you've believed and declare the truth. Then receive His peace, His forgiveness, His love, and His truth for your life.

ENDNOTE

1. www.etymonline.com; s.v. "worry" and "anxious." Accessed May 2008.

Chapter 4

A ROYAL FLUSH

REVIEWING THE PAST

Whenever we review the events of our lives apart from the blood of Jesus, we subject ourselves to the influence of the spirit of deception. In reality, my sinful past no longer exists (Vallotton, 51).

MPUTEES commonly experience something called "phantom" pain or sensation, where their nervous system and brain mistakenly interpret that certain physical signals are being sent by a limb that is no longer attached to the body. The memories of your sinful past can be like those phantom pains, only it's a little trickier because at your conversion you didn't just lose a part of you; you *literally died* and *were raised from the dead.* This is how Paul describes what happened to us at conversion:

> *Therefore we were buried with Him through baptism into death, that just as Christ was raised from the dead by the glory of the Father, even so we also should walk in newness of life. For if we have been united together in the likeness of His death, certainly we also shall be in the likeness of His resurrection, knowing this, that our old man was crucified with Him, that the body of sin might be done away with, that we should no longer be slaves of sin. For he who has died has been freed from sin* (Romans 6:4-7).

So how you do you retrain your brain to *think* and *remember* in accordance with that new reality? There are a number of truths that we all need to interact with regularly so that the reality of our conversion becomes established in our thinking and manifests fully in our behavior. This will hopefully be familiar territory, but invite the Holy Spirit to make it fresh and unveil new layers of this great, mysterious salvation we've received, and to take that revelation beyond mere head knowledge into a deeper level of freedom and power.

Let's review some of the Scriptures that discuss the truth that our sinful past no longer exists. Consider what Peter declared to the people after healing the lame man at the Beautiful Gate:

Repent therefore and be converted, that your sins may be blotted out... (Acts 3:19).

The record of our sinful past is blotted out—completely erased—when we repent and are converted. Scripture also puts it another way. It tells us that at our conversion we entered into a covenant with God through the blood of Jesus, and that one of the foundational realities of this covenant, prophesied by Jeremiah, was:

*Their sins and their lawless deeds **I will remember no more*** (Hebrews 10:17).

If our sin has been blotted out and forgotten by God, then what are we to do with our memories? How do we review our past *through* the blood of Jesus and not apart from it? As we have seen throughout this study, it comes down to choosing one of two perspectives on reality:

> The devil keeps records of our past. Yet those records are powerless without our agreement. He is the *accuser of the brethren*, but Jesus is our defender. We make an agreement with the accuser whenever we look at our past apart from the blood. When we agree with the devil, we empower him. When he is empowered, he devours. On the other hand, agreeing with God empowers us. It frees us from the power of a lie and enables us to live according to the will of God. This empowerment is not independent of God; it is empowerment *because* of God. When we agree with God we step into the power of truth, the momentum of the Cross (Vallotton, 51).

The devil remembers our sin. God has forgotten it. "When God views a believer's history like that, who are we to do otherwise?" (Vallotton, 55) We have a choice to do either, and in doing so to agree with a spiritual reality—one heavenly, and one hellish—that will manifest in our lives. Which one are you going to choose?

Does forgetting your sin sound like an impossible task? It is, without the empowerment of God. But when you decide to agree with God's perspective on your sin, He gives you the grace to forget that which seems unforgettable. He also gives you grace to remember that which is most true about you. Consider the following scriptures that address what we are to forget and what we are not to forget:

*But one thing I do, **forgetting those things which are behind** and reaching forward to those things which are ahead, I press toward the goal for the prize of the upward call of God in Christ Jesus* (Philippians 3:13-14).

*Bless the Lord, O my soul, and **forget not all His benefits**: who forgives all your iniquities...He has not dealt with us according to our sins, nor punished us according to our iniquities. For as the heavens are high above the earth, so great is His mercy toward those who fear Him; as far as the east is from the west, so far has He removed our transgressions from us* (Psalm 103:2-3, 10-12).

Like Paul, we are to forget the *past*, but we are to remember the *benefits* of the Lord—particularly the fact that He has forgiven *all* of our sin. Remember, that which we focus on becomes our reality. To forget our sin successfully, we must *fill our minds* with the reality of being forgiven.

❧ Take a moment to remember and list some of the benefits of God in your life.

The benefits of God that you have experienced in your life are always embedded in testimonies—the stories of what God has done in you and for you. These testimonies are your *real* history.

_____

_____

_____

_____

Forgiveness, in effect, changes the past...The blood actually changes our history into His story...Such is the love of God. What was despised becomes a testimony of God's grace—a thing of beauty! (Vallotton, 54-55)

❧ Describe one situation in your life where God has changed your history into His story through His forgiveness. How has He made something beautiful out of that which is despised?

_____

_____

_____

RECKONING

The renewing of the mind begins with our new identity obtained at the Cross. We were once slaves of sin, but are now slaves of righteousness. Our thought life must support that reality. The apostle Paul emphasized this in his letter to the church at Rome, saying, "Even so, think of yourself dead to sin" (Vallotton, 56).

Romans 6:11 gives us a specific key for establishing an agreement with what is in God's mind when it comes to what the blood of Jesus accomplished. Another version puts it this way:

> Likewise you also, **reckon** yourselves to be dead indeed to sin, but alive to God in Christ Jesus our Lord (Romans 6:11).

The word translated "reckon" in this verse is the Greek word *logizomai*.[1] It means, "to count, calculate, to take into account and to weigh the reasons." The entry for this word in Strong's Concordance makes the note, "This word deals with reality. If I reckon (*logizomai*) that my bank book has $25 in it, it has $25 in it. Otherwise I am deceiving myself. This word refers more to fact than supposition or opinion."

The first step in establishing an agreement with God is to take the evidence into account and arrive at the following conclusion: *I am dead to sin and alive to God.* And according to Paul, the evidence that we are to take into account *is not our individual behavior.* It is what Jesus did on the Cross. Consider a few of the main points Paul presented in the passage we saw at the beginning of this study, along with a few others in the book of Romans:

Jesus' blood fully atoned for our sin (see Rom. 3:25).

What are some of the implications of this fact?

_____

_____

_____

By putting our faith in Christ to redeem us through this atonement, we are justified before God and righteousness is imputed to us (see Rom. 3:22,24).

What are some of the implications of this fact?

_____

_____

_____

When we were baptized into Christ, we were baptized into His death. Because we died, we are free from sin (see Rom. 6:3,7).

What are some of the implications of this fact?

_____

_____

_____

The New Testament is filled with other statements like this that we must chew on, understand, and set up like pillars in our minds. Establishing this foundation of evidence in our thinking is vital if we are to step fully into a righteous lifestyle:

> When we are charged to think of ourselves dead to sin, it is more than a suggestion to think positively about our conversion. It is an invitation to step into the momentum of a reality made available only through the Cross. *The supernatural power released in this way of thinking is what creates a lifestyle of freedom.* It is able

to do this because it is *Truth*. To say that I have sinned is true. To say that I am free of sin is truer still (Vallotton, 56).

❧ What are some truths from Scripture about who you are because of your conversion that you have established in your thinking? Where in your life do you see that believing these truths enabled you to step into a dimension of supernatural power that you didn't experience before?

_____

_____

_____

_____

❧ What happens when we get stuck on the first truth—"I have sinned"—and never move on to the higher truth? What kind of reality and supernatural power does that truth release into our lives?

_____

_____

_____

_____

Consider:

To maintain consciousness of our sinful past to help us become more humble is the cruelty of a religious spirit; *it requires us to keep something in our minds that isn't in God's.* In reality, it is much more humbling to live in the liberty of unearned forgiveness. When we are forgiven, the King gives us permission to live as though we had never sinned (Vallotton, 52).

❧ The idea that we have been given permission to live as though we had never sinned was also expressed in Chapter 3 of *The Supernatural Ways of Royalty*: "Forgiveness restores the standard" (Vallotton, 46). What does living as though you had never sinned look like? What is the standard that has been restored in our lives?

_____

_____

_____

_____

❧ Why is it humbling to live in the liberty of unearned forgiveness? What are some things that may be holding you back from living in that freedom and responsibility?

_____

_____

_____

_____

HOW SHALL WE THEN LIVE?

After we undertake this process of "reckoning" that we are dead to sin, the second step in establishing an agreement with God is to start to act according to what we believe. It is as we demonstrate our trust in the truth by stepping out in obedience that we put the supernatural power available to us to work. We see this progression in Romans 6 as well. After Paul tells us to "reckon" ourselves dead to sin, he declares:

> *Therefore do not let sin reign in your mortal body, that you should obey it in its lusts. And do not present your members as instruments of unrighteousness to sin, but present yourselves to God as being alive from the dead, and your members as instruments of righteousness to God* (Romans 6:12-13).

☞ What does it mean to present yourself to God as being alive from the dead?

_____

_____

_____

☞ What does it mean to present your bodies to God as instruments of righteousness?

_____

_____

_____

You'll notice that Paul doesn't tell us that being dead to sin and being free from sin do not mean that we *cannot* sin. Precisely because we are *free*, we have a *choice*. At first, it doesn't seem realistic that God would entrust us, former slaves who don't have a clue about handling freedom, with that level of liberty. But that's where our understanding of what the Cross did and the grace we have received through it needs to expand. The blood didn't just cover our past mistakes; it covered all our moments of stumbling as we learn how to live as free sons and daughters. So there are two things we need to do when we stumble.

The first thing we need to do is to confess our sin. The apostle John said:

> *If we say that we have no sin, we deceive ourselves, and the truth is not in us. If we confess our sins, He is faithful and just to forgive us our sins and to cleanse us from all unrighteousness. If we say that we have not sinned, we make Him a liar, and His word is not in us....My little children, these things I write to you, so that you may not sin. And if anyone sins, we have an Advocate with the Father, Jesus Christ the righteous. And He Himself is the propitiation for our sins, and not for ours only but also for the whole world* (1 John 1:8-10; 2:1-2).

The very Person who professionally dealt with the issue of sin is our personal lawyer. No one knows how to deal with sin better, and He's fully committed to cleaning us up every single time we fall down. There's never going to be a point where He gives up on us.

❧ How quick are you to run to Jesus when you make a mistake? Does confessing your sin come hard or easy for you? What do you believe is God's attitude towards you when you make a mistake?

_____

_____

_____

The second thing we need to do, after we confess our sin, is to be reminded of who we are becoming in God. We have been "predestined to be conformed to the image of His Son" (Rom. 8:29). God is not going to stop refining and developing us until we are mature sons and daughters who perfectly reflect the nature of Jesus Christ. And the biggest things that tie us to our future in God are His *promises*. Peter states:

> *His divine power has given to us all things that pertain to life and godliness, through the knowledge of Him who called us by glory and virtue, by which have been given to us **exceedingly great and precious promises, that through these you may be partakers of the divine nature**... (2 Peter 1:3-4).*

We partake of the divine nature—the nature we are called to display—*through* the promises of God. Consider:

> Promises are like the rudder of a ship. Rudders determine the direction of that ship. And what I do with God's promises determines the direction of my thought-life, and eventually affects my reality. It is essential to understand what God thinks of me (and others) in order to step into my destiny. Regardless of circumstances, God's word is true. "Let God be found true, though every man be found a liar" (Romans 3:4). Again, *we cannot afford to think differently about ourselves than God does* (Vallotton, 57).

Through Isaiah, God declared the following:

> *"For **My thoughts are not your thoughts,** nor are your ways My ways," says the Lord. "For as the heavens are higher than the earth, so are My ways higher than your ways, and My thoughts than your thoughts. For as the rain comes down, and*

the snow from heaven, and do not return there, but water the earth, and make it bring forth and bud, that it may give seed to the sower and bread to the eater, so shall My word be that goes forth from My mouth; it shall not return to Me void, but it shall accomplish what I please, and it shall prosper in the thing for which I sent it (Isaiah 55:8-11).

In essence, this prophecy declares that *God's thoughts and God's ways are superior to ours, and they have the power to change our reality as they bring Heaven to earth.* The promises of God reveal His thoughts and His ways to us, and so we must anchor our minds in this reality.

Interestingly, Jesus called the Holy Spirit "the Promise" (Luke 24:49). He explained that the Holy Spirit's assignment in the life of every believer is to guide us "into all truth" by personally *declaring* the word of the Lord—the word that cannot return void—into our lives (see John 16:13). The Holy Spirit, the Promise, is the One who imparts the divine nature of God to us as He declares the promises of God over us. This is why our relationship with the Holy Spirit, as it was for Jesus, is the absolute center of our lives as believers.

CONCLUSION

Take some time to speak with the Holy Spirit and ask Him to speak to you about the promises of God over your life. You may want to spend time reviewing prophetic words or promises from Scripture that have been spoken over you in the past and ask the Lord how He wants to lead you toward their fulfillment. Lean into His voice—He is always speaking His thoughts over you and they're all good!

ENDNOTE

1. Strong's Concordance, taken from http://cf.blueletterbible.org/lang/lexicon/lexicon.cfm?Strongs=G3049&t=KJV; accessed May 2008, s.v. "logizomai."

Chapter 5

LIZARDS IN THE PALACE

WHAT'S IN A NAME?

We respond to our environment according to the way we see ourselves. Words spoken to us become names that we carry in our hearts. These names paint a portrait of us in our imagination and become the lenses through which we view our world. Sticks and stones are breaking our bones, but names are taking away our future!...It is so important that we live by our God-given names and not by the names that tie us to bondage (Vallotton, 62-63).

❧ What are some of the names, either positive or negative, that have been given to you throughout your life? How have these names affected the way that you perceive yourself and respond to your environment?

_____

_____

_____

_____

_____

❧ Do any of these names contradict what God says about you as His son or daughter? If so, can you recognize if these names are still powerful in your life and whether they are keeping you in bondage? Where do you see those names at work in your life the most?

_____

_____

_____

New Name, New Destiny

Can you imagine fighting with an angel all night long, getting thrashed, and letting him go just because he called you by a nickname?...You would if you understood the revelation Jacob had. His new name "Israel" meant "a prince of God." The name released him into his prophetic destiny...A prophetic declaration is more than mere words, because it releases grace to accomplish what it says (Vallotton, 63-64).

Why and how does a prophetic declaration release grace upon us? Jesus gave us one of the clearest explanations for this when He expressed the following spiritual principle:

> *For out of the abundance of the heart the mouth speaks. A good man out of the good treasure of his heart brings forth good things, and an evil man out of the evil treasure brings forth evil things* (Matthew 12:34b-35).

We've already looked at the principle of Proverbs 4:23—*the issues of life flow from the heart* (see Prov. 4:23). Our hearts are the spiritual centers of our beings, the seats of our desires, thoughts, and beliefs. The heart is the dimension of life that interacts most immediately with the spirit realm, and it is the heart's communion with either heavenly or hellish thoughts, desires, and perspectives that determines what kind of spiritual power is released through our lives to shape our reality.

As Jesus explained, our *words* release the reality of our *hearts*. We "bring forth" either good things or evil things as our words unlock the treasures of our hearts. So what happens when God speaks in a prophetic declaration? It releases the treasure of His heart, the power of His very being and nature, which is also His *grace*, into our lives. Grace (*charis*) is more than God's unmerited favor. It is the *operational power* of God.

So what is the significance of God declaring a name over you? What's in a name? Consider:

> When the Lord met me and told me I was a pauper who had become a prince, He was giving me a name change. Once I knew my new name, I had access to the grace I needed to begin walking in a new identity. It is vital that we all hear the name that the Lord has given to us and allow that name to define our identities (Vallotton, 64-65).

The scriptural treatment of names is a little foreign to us in our culture, where we are mostly unfamiliar with what most names mean. But names in Scripture are always meaningful, and by and large they signify two primary aspects of a person's identity—*relationship* and *nature*. When God declares a name over you, He is releasing the grace for you to mature in your relationship with Him, and to be expanded in your nature so that you can be more like Him. Or more specifically, when God releases His grace into your life, He is actually releasing *Himself,* and when He releases Himself into you—if you receive Him—your life cannot become anything but a greater expression of who He is.

What is one of the names that God has spoken over your life through Scripture, prophetic words, or any of the other many ways He speaks? What does this name signify when it comes to your nature and/or your relationship with Him? How has this name changed the way you see yourself and the way you behave?

_____

_____

_____

_____

_____

BEING BEFORE DOING

You have to be a human being before you are a human doing. When we try to "do" something without first "being" someone, we usually find ourselves making a living at a job we hate. Another ramification of this failure to discover true identity is that many people learn to derive their self-esteem from what they *do*. This may seem fine for a while if they can perform well. When they can't perform anymore, for whatever reason, their self-esteem goes into the pit (Vallotton, 66).

✎ Have you experienced these things in your life: low self-esteem related to failure to perform well, or discouragement in an unfulfilling career? If so, how have you dealt with these situations? Would you say that these experiences are related to the issue of identity, and if so, how?

_____

_____

_____

The truth about all of us as human beings is twofold: first, none of us thought ourselves up or brought ourselves into existence; and second, we are all searching for our identities and the purpose for our existence. As we interact with our world and the people around us, we all take on various roles and identities. But the truth is that the Person who thought us up and made us in the first place, is the only One who can tell us who we really are. And what happens when He does that? Consider what the Lord said to Israel through the prophet Isaiah:

But now, thus says the Lord, who created you, O Jacob, and He who formed you, O Israel: "Fear not, for I have redeemed you; I have called you by your name; you are Mine" (Isaiah 43:1).

When the Person who thought us up in the first place calls to us, the primary thing He wants us to know is *who He is* and *what He has done for us.* He has *redeemed* us, He has *named* us, and *we belong to Him.* Our identity all flows from our relationship with Him.

Now, since none of us have a true identity apart from God, it's no surprise that until we come to Him, most of us experience a life described in the quote above—a life defined by what we *do*, which is usually not congruent with who we were designed to *be*. So when we come to Christ, we have to make a big switch in our thinking—not only a switch to defining ourselves according to who God is and what He has done instead of what we do, but a switch from thinking that our identity flows from our behavior. We've had it backward all this time—*our being does not flow from our doing, but rather our doing flows from our being.*

Obviously, one of our main concerns at conversion is to change our behavior—to stop sinning. But one of the over-arching themes of the Bible is that the sin issue cannot be dealt with on the level of behavior. We must be changed in our *nature* and in our *relationship* with God first—and this is precisely what the Cross did. This is why we need a new name, and it is why we receive that name before we can start to act congruently with that new identity. If we don't receive that name change, we will be stuck in the identity of our old names:

> The word "sinner" implies that we are prone to do wrong. If we believe that we are sinners, we will sin by faith! Remember…"For as [a man] thinks within himself, so he is" (Proverbs 23:7). Like Jacob, trapped in deception by his name, if we still believe we are sinners, we will be unable to access the grace to live as a saint and will still try to perform good works in order to merit forgiveness (Vallotton, 67).

🙢 Have there been periods in your life as a Christian in which you have struggled to break out of a pattern of sinful behavior? How has learning to walk in freedom from sin in your life been connected to embracing the identity of a saint?

_____

_____

_____

_____

_____

_____

In your experience, has the Church reinforced the idea that we as believers are sinners, or saints? Has it reinforced the idea that we are forgiven, or that we must try harder to be good in order to merit forgiveness? How has either of these perspectives influenced the culture of believers where you fellowship? How does a particular belief about our identity as believers shape our expectations of one another?

_____

_____

_____

_____

_____

_____

_____

LITTLE CHRISTS

Earlier you answered a question about the words that God has personally spoken over your life. It is vitally important that we receive these personal words from the Lord—they are part of having a real relationship with Him. But we also need to be aware of the names that we all share as members of the Body of Christ. These names are the foundation stones of our identity and shape how we relate to God and one another. So what is the new name that God has given to us as believers?

Consider:

We are Christians; it is not our nature to do wrong. Our very nature has been changed. Now we are actually saints; righteousness is part of our new nature and it is natural for us to glorify God. Our old man is buried. We need to stop visiting our tombs and talking to our dead, old man...We are a new creation. It's below our nature to act like that now—we are now princes and princesses of the King!...We are Saints, holy believers, and Christians, which means we are "little

Christs!" When the Father looks at us, He sees the image of the Son He loves
(Vallotton, 68, 72).

What is the significance of being a *Christian*—a "little Christ"? It means that God has given
us a new name—a name that carries a new identity, a new nature, and a new relationship with
Him—and that name is *Christ*. Paul expressed this exchange of his old identity for the identity
of Christ when he said:

> *I have been crucified with Christ; it is no longer I who live, but Christ lives in me;*
> *and the life which I now live in the flesh I live by faith in the Son of God, Who loved*
> *me and gave Himself for me* (Galatians 2:20).

Paul also said:

> *For you are all sons of God through faith in Christ Jesus. For as many of you as were*
> *baptized into Christ have put on Christ. There is neither Jew nor Greek, there is*
> *neither slave nor free, there is neither male nor female; for you are all one in Christ*
> *Jesus* (Galatians 3:26-28).

He reiterated this idea again in Colossians:

> *You have put off the old man with his deeds, and have put on the new man who is*
> *renewed in knowledge according to the image of Him who created him, where there*
> *is neither Greek nor Jew, circumcised nor uncircumcised, barbarian, Scythian, slave*
> *nor free, but Christ is all and in all* (Colossians 3:9-11).

In other words, all the things that used to define us before we came to Christ—our ethnic-
ity, gender, religion, or economic status—can no longer do so. The only thing that defines us
now is the Person of Jesus Christ. Remember, this name defines our *relationship* to God and our
nature. In the verses from Galatians, Paul says that because we have "put Christ on" through
baptism, we now stand in the same relation to the Father as He does. We are sons. And in
Colossians, he says that we have put on "the new man", Christ, and thus our nature is a reflection of the One who created us.

The idea that the old things that used to define us are no longer relevant, not only has significant implications for how we see ourselves before God, but how we see one another. When we look at another believer, we are to see Christ, for "Christ is all and in all." And thus, we should treat one another as we would treat Christ. In fact, in the parable of the sheep and the goats, Jesus declares that the way we treat believers *is* how we are treating Him (see Matt. 25). So the question is, how are you treating Christ in your spiritual brothers and sisters? How would remembering Christ in them change your behavior?

_____

_____

_____

_____

_____

IN HIS NAME

The name *Christ* means "anointed."[1] The apostle Peter explained the nature of the anointing upon Jesus' life thus:

> *God anointed Jesus of Nazareth with the Holy Spirit and with power...* (Acts 10:38).

Likewise, the anointing of the Holy Spirit and power is *the key* to walking in our identity as little Christs, as sons of God. As Paul said,

> *For as many as are led by the Spirit of God, these are sons of God* (Romans 8:14).

What does it look like to be led by the Spirit of God? It means looking like Jesus. Or, as Jesus put it, one of the things it means is to do things "in His name." We are to baptize people *in His name*. We are to ask the Father for things *in His name*. We are to gather *in His name*. When we do things *in His name*, we are literally doing what Christ *would* do—and actually *is* doing—in the situation. And when we do things in His name, the Holy Spirit is the One anointing us to do them. Peter made the following connection in this regard:

> *...If you are reproached for the **name of Christ**, blessed are you, for **the Spirit of glory and of God** rests upon you...* (1 Peter 4:14).

It is the Spirit of God resting upon us that clothes us with the ability to do things in the name of Christ. The evidence of this is that we evoke the same kind of responses from those around us that Jesus evoked through His ministry, including reproach.

Describe a couple of things you have done in the name of Jesus. What were the results of these actions?

_____

_____

_____

_____

_____

_____

_____

_____

The Book of Acts records how the early believers received the anointing of the Holy Spirit and began to do things in the name of Jesus. After Pentecost, the first thing we read about is the healing of the lame man at the Beautiful Gate, which Peter explained thus:

> *So when Peter saw it, he responded to the people: "Men of Israel, why do you marvel at this? Or why look so intently at us, as though by our own power or godliness we had made this man walk? The God of Abraham, Isaac, and Jacob, the God of our fathers, glorified His Servant Jesus...And **His name, through faith in His name,** has made this man strong, whom you see and know. Yes, **the faith which comes through Him** has given him this perfect soundness in the presence of you all"* (Acts 3:12-13,16).

This statement reveals some of the dimensions of what it means for us to do things in His name. It's not a matter of saying the name of Jesus, or even a matter of trying to do the things that Jesus did. It comes down to receiving *the faith that comes through Him,* which is something we only have access to if we are in relationship *with* Him.

Conclusion

In John 16, Jesus explained to His disciples that when He ascended to the Father and the Father sent the Holy Spirit, the Holy Spirit's job was to tell them everything that Jesus was saying. In doing so, He was promising that we would have access to the same source from which Jesus' ministry flowed. The key to Jesus' ministry was that He did everything He saw His Father do and said what His Father said. The Holy Spirit enables us to hear and see what Jesus is doing so that we can know Him, become like Him, and partner with Him in what He's doing. Then we can truly bear His name and do things in His name.

Spend some time today asking the Holy Spirit to quicken the eyes and ears of your heart to hear and see what Jesus is doing and draw you more deeply into communion with Him.

Endnote

1. Strong's Greek, accessed May 2008, taken from http://cf.blueletterbible.org/lang/lexicon/lexicon.cfm?Strongs=G5547&t=KJV; s.v. "Christ."

Chapter 6

TRAINING FOR REIGNING

RAISED TO RULE

Imagine you had been raised in a palace where every person around you told you that you were destined to be a king or queen from birth. Who would you be today and how would your life be different now? Maybe it would be easier to envision being brought up as the President of the United States. Think about the ramifications of your childhood and how it could affect your destiny (Vallotton, 74).

SPEND some time doing this exercise. Decide which role would be easier for you to envision—a king or queen, or the President. Then imagine how certain areas of your life would be affected if you had been brought up to walk in this role. First, list some of the attitudes and beliefs about yourself that you think your parents and teachers would want to see you develop in your life.

_____

_____

_____

_____

_____

Now, take some time to jot down how you might be raised to think and behave in the following areas in order to achieve greatness as a leader:

Physical health:

_____

_____

_____

Education:

_____

_____

_____

Marriage and Family:

_____

_____

_____

Finance:

_____

_____

_____

Work:

_____

_____

_____

❧ What are some of the differences in the mindsets and behaviors you described above and the mindsets and behaviors you observe in your own life?

_____

_____

_____

WHAT KIND OF RULERS ARE WE?

Of course, there are many different kinds of rulers and many different kinds of kingdoms. This is why we need to know what our King and His Kingdom are like if we are going to succeed in becoming the kind of rulers He has called us to be. The point is that our heavenly Father, the King, has called us "kings and priests" (Rev. 1:6). This identity is given to us now and for eternity. We may not all be destined to be the President of the United States. But this is what we are destined to do:

> _For if by the one man's offense death reigned through the one, much more those who receive abundance of grace and of the gift of righteousness will reign in life through the One, Jesus Christ_ (Romans 5:17).

In Christ, through His grace, every believer is called to reign in life. One of the things this implies is that we are not to be victims of our temporary circumstances. Instead, we are to experience and display the victorious life of the Kingdom of our God to everyone around us. We are to see and think from the reality of the eternal Kingdom of God toward the situations in our lives.

❧ What does it mean to have an eternal perspective? What are the things that we do in our lives that really matter in the long run? How do these priorities influence your daily decisions?

_____

_____

_____

_____

_____

People who live "from eternity" do things differently than most people, because their priorities are different. Consider what C.S. Lewis said about what matters in the long run:

> Christianity asserts that every individual human being is going to live forever, and this must be either true or false. Now there are a good many things which would not be worth bothering about if I were going to live only seventy years, but which I had better bother about very seriously if I am going to live for ever. Perhaps my bad temper or my jealousy are gradually getting worse—so gradually that the increase in seventy years will not be very noticeable. But it might be absolute hell in a million years: in fact, if Christianity is true, Hell is the precisely correct technical term for what it would be. And immortality makes this other difference...If individuals live only seventy years, then a state, or a nation, or a civilisation, which may last for a thousand years, is more important than an individual. But if Christianity is true, then the individual is not only more important but incomparably more important, for he is everlasting and the life of a state or a civilization, compared with his, is only a moment.[1]

People are what matter in the long run, and thus people—all people—are the priority of Heaven. What is Heaven's agenda for people? It is simply *life*—the true life that can only be found in the Kingdom of God. Our Father paid the highest price He could pay for every person on the planet to experience *eternal life*. Jesus said:

> *...I have come that they may have life, and that they may have it more abundantly* (John 10:10).

Later, He explained what eternal life is:

> *And this is eternal life, that they may know You, the only true God, and Jesus Christ whom You have sent* (John 17:3).

Kingdom life, eternal life, flows directly from knowing God personally. Our relationship with God is the key to "reigning in life," because it is in coming to know Him that we come to know who we are, what our purpose in life is, and how to walk it out. As we align our thinking and behavior with who He is, the supernatural life of His kingdom begins to flow through our lives, enabling us to do what we could not otherwise do.

What does this tell us about our role as kings? It tells us that our top priorities are *knowing God* and *making Him known* to those around us. It also tells us that the primary thing that grooms us to rule and reign with our Father is our *relationship with Him*. We can be raised in a strong Christian family, go to a great ministry school, have lots of Christian friends, hear great sermons all the time and read our Bibles a lot, but we will only be successfully trained to look and act like our Father by knowing Him and maturing in our relationship with Him.

    What are some of the primary signs that a person knows God? What do these things tell you about the nature of eternal life?

_____

_____

_____

_____

SERVING

If we are called kings, then we are called to be leaders. A true leader is always thinking about others. A person may have a great vision, but if no one is following, then he or she is not a leader. True leaders must have vision, because they are leading people *toward* something. As representatives of the Kingdom of God, we have been called to lead people *into* that Kingdom.

But the question of *how* we lead people is just as important to God as *where* we are leading them. In order to answer this question, we must look to our model King and Priest, Jesus Christ, who manifested Heaven's priority for people, and whose leadership was the most revolutionary in history—even to His disciples. The Gospels record that Jesus' disciples recognized Him as a King and anticipated that they would get to share some kind of leadership role with Him. They had several discussions about who was the greatest among them, asking Jesus to grant them certain positions in His Kingdom. But Jesus blew their minds when He defined the role of a prince in His Father's Kingdom:

But Jesus called them to Himself and said, "You know that the rulers of the Gentiles lord it over them, and those who are great exercise authority over them. Yet it shall not be so among you; but whoever desires to become great among you, let him be your servant. And whoever desires to be first among you, let him be your slave—just as the Son of Man did not come to be served, but to serve, and to give His life a ransom for many" (Matthew 20:25-28).

Paul expounded on this kind of leadership to the Philippians:

Let nothing be done through selfish ambition or conceit, but in lowliness of mind let each esteem others better than himself. Let each of you look out not only for his own interests, but also for the interests of others. Let this mind be in you which was also in Christ Jesus, who, being in the form of God, did not consider it robbery to be equal with God, but made Himself of no reputation, taking the form of a bondservant, and coming in the likeness of men. And being found in appearance as a man, He humbled Himself and became obedient to the point of death, even the death of the cross (Philippians 2:3-8).

These passages pretty much contradict every bit of the world's wisdom on becoming a great leader. But let's focus on one implication of Paul's words. The word *esteem* in Philippians 2:3 means both "to consider" and "to be a leader", even in particular to be "a prince, of regal power."[2] If we consider how these two definitions might work together, it seems fairly obvious to conclude that *esteeming* each other better than ourselves means considering each other to have a higher position of authority and honor. And upon what basis can we make this consideration?

Throughout this study we have been giving attention to the fact that we must embrace the new identity God gave us at conversion. Along with embracing the revelation that *you* are a prince or princess of God, there is another revelation that we must all have. The revelation is that everyone around us in the Body of Christ is also royalty. It is largely this revelation that will enable us to "esteem others better than" ourselves.

✥ Here is another imaginative exercise for you. You've already imagined what you might be like if you had been raised with the idea that you were destined for greatness. Now it's time to imagine what it would be like to be raised with the idea that you were destined to serve a great person. Pick someone you admire and write down some of the attitudes, priorities, and behaviors you would need to develop to serve that person.

_____

_____

_____

✥ Now imagine that the person you have been called to serve hasn't actually achieved greatness yet. Maybe he or she actually looks more like a failure or someone without potential at all. What are some of the challenges you might face in fulfilling your role? What would you need to do it well?

_____

_____

_____

THE INTERESTS OF OTHERS

This is the true mentality of a prince or princess. They spend more time raising up people around them rather than worrying about their own significance. They already know who they are inside, which enables them to become selfless and give out more than they receive (Vallotton, 77).

This kind of servant leadership, modeled perfectly by our King, Jesus, is the place of maturity at the end of this journey of believing and walking out our royal identity. We've been trying to use our imaginations to envision this place of maturity because our journey largely begins in the mind. As Paul pointed out, we are to let "this mind" be in us, which was in Christ, and we are to "esteem" or "consider" others better than ourselves (see Phil. 2:5-6). We not only have to learn to see ourselves differently, we have to learn to see those around us differently.

One of the things we have to see is that God has designed His body in such a way that we are interdependent. As a result, the process of maturity in each of our lives is intimately tied up in a process of giving and receiving grace to one another, particularly through our words. Paul describes this maturing process in Ephesians 4:

> *That we...speaking the truth in love, may grow up in all things into Him Who is the Head—Christ—from whom the whole body, joined and knit together by what every joint supplies, according to the effective working by which each part does its share, causes growth of the body for the edifying of itself in love* (Ephesians 4:14-16).

❧ What does it mean to speak the truth in love? Why do you suppose that it is such a vital part of the maturing process of the Body of Christ?

_____

_____

_____

_____

_____

As princes and princesses, we are not only called to honor others before ourselves. We are supposed to make a contribution to others' lives that will enable them to fulfill their potential in God. Consider:

Just like (King) Saul, we all have gifts, talents and abilities; yet some of us don't believe in our potential until someone else comes alongside us and says, "Look at how much is inside of you." Many of us have lost our true selves in the garbage of our lives. We, the church, are commissioned to develop a princely prophetic culture that causes people's destinies to be revealed. People will then be changed back into the people they were designed to be when God conceived them...As the Royal Priesthood of God, we are called to develop a culture in our homes, churches, businesses, and ultimately in nations that brings out the best in individuals, facilitating their princely destinies. We do this by seeing and treating others and ourselves not as we are, but as God created us to be. This knowledge and love can only come out of intimacy with God. No longer are we His slaves, but His friends, walking by His side as kings and queens of His court (Vallotton, 80, 84).

☙ Where does the ability to *see* the truth about one another and then *speak that truth in love* come from? How can you grow in that ability?

_____

_____

_____

_____

☙ Describe a situation in your life in which you felt like the best of you came to the surface. What were the circumstances or influences that brought that out of you? How can you be intentional about doing that for others?

_____

_____

_____

_____

❧ What does it look like to treat people not as they are but as God created them to be? How has your intimacy with God enabled you to do this?

_____

_____

_____

_____

CONCLUSION

Spend some time chewing the passages from Matthew and Philippians that describe Jesus' model of princely servanthood. Ask the Holy Spirit to show you areas in your life in which you can embrace the mind of Christ more fully.

ENDNOTES

1. C.S. Lewis, *Mere Christianity* (New York, NY: Harper-Collins, 1972), 74-75.

2. Strong's Concordance, taken from http://cf.blueletterbible.org/lang/lexicon/lexicon.cfm?Strongs=G3049 &t=KJV; accessed May 2008; s.v. "esteem."

Chapter 7

GUESS WHO IS COMING TO DINNER?

FRIENDS OF THE FATHER

You are My friends if you do whatever I command you. No longer do I call you servants, for a servant does not know what his master is doing; but I have called you friends, for all things that I have heard from My Father I have made known to you (John 15:14-15).

CONSIDER the different sides of the friendship that Jesus described in this passage. He said that our part of friendship is expressed in our obedience to His commands, and that His part of friendship is expressed in letting us know what the Father is saying and doing. If these were the only verses where we could learn about friendship with God, I wonder if we would think there is much difference between a slave obeying his master's commands and Jesus' friends obeying His commands.

But perhaps we can understand Jesus' version of friendship with God more by looking at the following verses:

*Jesus said to them, "**My food is to do the will of Him who sent Me,** and to finish His work"* (John 4:34).

*For I have come down from heaven, **not to do My own will, but the will of Him who sent me*** (John 6:38).

Therefore when He (Christ) came into the world, He said: "Sacrifice and offering You did not desire, but a body You have prepared for Me. In burnt offerings and sacrifices for sin You had no pleasure. Then I said, 'Behold, I have come—in the volume of the book it is written of Me—to do Your will, O God'" (Hebrews 10:5-7).

What do these verses indicate about the nature of Jesus' friendship with the Father? How is Jesus' relationship with the Father similar to the version of friendship that He described to us? How is Jesus' version of friendship similar to His version of leadership?

_____

_____

_____

We can see from these verses that in stating that His friends are those who obey His commands, Jesus was not laying upon them any heavier burden than He Himself carries in His friendship with God. He perfectly modeled the obedience that He asks of us. But notice that obedience is not the only thing that qualifies us as friends:

> Jesus...reminds us that although slaves obey out of fear, friends obey the Father out of love. A willing heart is a prerequisite to moving out of slavery into friendship. He also highlights the fact that slaves do not know what their master is doing but friends know all about the Father's business (Vallotton, 85-86).

True friends *know what the other friend is doing*. This is the key to understanding why Jesus obeyed the Father and why Jesus' friends will obey His commands. If we connect the fact that friends obey to the fact that friends are those with inside access to what God is doing, a sensible conclusion is that *the obedience of a friend is actually a **response** to the personal disclosure offered by the one with whom he or she is in friendship*. The "willing heart" of the friend can really only be expressed because he or she has been entrusted with inside information about what matters to the person he or she cares about.

However, a willing heart has to be present in a person if he or she is going to be able to perceive the overtures of friendship—that is, the revelation—that God is offering, and come to be someone who knows what the Father is saying and doing. Look at what Jesus said to those who were trying to discern whether what He was saying and doing really was the revelation of the Father's heart and will:

*My doctrine is not Mine, but His who sent Me. **If anyone wills to do His will**, he shall know concerning the doctrine, whether it is from God or whether I speak on My own authority* (John 7:16-17).

A willing heart, as we see here and in the verses above, is specifically a heart that is willing to submit to the will of God. It is this willing heart that in fact determines our ability to discern what God is saying in the many ways that He speaks, and respond to it.

    ❧ Have you ever received a word from God that you didn't really understand but responded to in obedience anyway? Or, have you ever felt prompted to do something and done it, only to realize later that it was God speaking to you? What has the fruit of this obedience been in your life? How has it brought you into greater revelation and intimacy with God?

_____

_____

_____

Notice that in the John 15 passage Jesus makes a point of stating conclusively that for His part, He communicated *everything* He heard from His Father. This expresses the heart of God in friendship with us. He desires to withhold nothing from us.

Scripture records the fact that God speaks to man in many different ways. Jesus explained some of the reason for speaking the way He did when His disciples asked Him why He spoke in parables. In essence, He said that by communicating truth in parables, those who did not have the heart to seek for understanding would stay as ignorant as they were before they heard the parables, while those with seeking hearts would have access to the mysteries of His kingdom (see Luke 8:10). As Bill Johnson often points out, God hides things *for* us, not *from* us. But He hides them so that those of us with willing hearts have a chance to participate in our end of the relationship. So, one question worth asking is, where do we get this willing heart? Consider:

*Restore to me the joy of Your salvation and sustain me with a **willing spirit*** (Psalm 51:12 NASB).

*Watch and pray, lest you enter into temptation. The **spirit indeed is willing**, but the flesh is weak* (Matthew 26:41).

The willing heart that enables us to walk in friendship with God originates in the spirit. As David's prayer to God in Psalm 51 models for us and as Jesus exhorted His disciples, prayer—that is, communication and intimacy with God in His presence—is the key to developing this "willing spirit" (see Ps. 51:12). God can give us this willing spirit because He has it and expressed it perfectly in the Person of Jesus Christ.

❧ As we see in Christ, a willing spirit is truly seen in the fact that a person actually does the will of God. A willing spirit is more than a good intention; it is a force in us that drives us to find out what God is doing and do it. Jesus said that doing what God was doing was His "food"—the thing that energized Him and fulfilled Him. Would you say that this spirit characterizes your life? How has spending time in the presence of God increased your ability and desire to do what He is doing? Have you experienced the fulfillment and energy that Jesus was talking about in doing what God is doing?

_____

_____

_____

WHERE DOES OBEDIENCE COME FROM?

Jesus set the example for us by doing what he saw the Father doing. If we are to do the same, we must realize that we have been invited to have the same kind of friendship with the Father that Jesus Himself had (Vallotton, 86).

Look at Jesus' own words concerning His relationship with His Father:

Then Jesus answered and said to them, "Most assuredly, I say to you, the Son can do nothing of Himself, but what He sees the Father do; for whatever He does, the Son also does in like manner. **For the Father loves the Son, and shows Him all things that He Himself does;** and He will show Him greater works than these, **that you may marvel**" (John 5:19-20).

There is a direct correlation here between the Father's love and the Father's revelation of what He's doing. There is also an intentional flow of the Father's love for people, displayed in His works, through the Son. This is one place we see that Jesus' relationship with the Father was not simply the heart of His ministry, it was a personal invitation from the Father to all those who would believe in Christ to come to know Him in the same way.

    ✤ It might take some of us a while to get used to the idea that God loves us in the same way that He loves Christ and has granted us complete access to know Him and partner with Him like Christ did. So here are some questions that may be good to ask yourself: Do I expect the Father to reveal Himself to me and show me all that He is doing? Do I expect Him to show me great works? If so, how do I demonstrate these expectations in my life? If not, where in my heart and mind am I missing the reality of the love of God in my life?

_____

_____

_____

Consider:

Unfortunately, the church has had a single-dimensional view of what it means to have a relationship with God. We have overemphasized obedience and underemphasized friendship. This has resulted in our interactions with the Almighty becoming robotic and soldier-like. Men and women of old understood something that, centuries later, we are still trying to figure out: God wants friends, not slaves! (Vallotton, 89)

The reality is that unless we understand God's heart of love for us and His desire for true, intimate friendship, we won't understand what Jesus is talking about when He says, "You are my friends if you do whatever I command you" (John 5:14). We will hear that all He cares about is obedience, and that He is telling us to prove our love for Him by doing what He wants. But if we understand what Jesus' relationship with His Father was like, the kind of relationship we've been invited into, we will be able to hear Him saying, "True obedience is simply the natural response from the heart of a friend, and it's simply doing what I'm doing."

If true obedience is doing and saying what God is doing and saying, then obedience necessarily flows from *being with God*. It's pretty hard to know what your friends are up to if you never spend time with them. Look at what Jesus says about the nature of His acts of obedience:

Do you not believe that I am in the Father, and the Father in Me? The words that I speak to you I do not speak on My own authority; but the Father who dwells in Me does the works (John 14:10).

Jesus' obedience is not something He did apart from the Father. True obedience in friendship with God is a partnership, but a partnership unlike any partnership we can observe here on earth. We must come to understand that obedience itself is not something we do alone, but is something we are doing with the Father, as well as something that the Father is doing through us. When our actions flow from our intimacy with God, and when we understand that we are doing them together with Him, serving God will be anything but "robotic and soldier-like."

&- Do you experience obedience as a partnership with God? Has serving God become "soldier-like" or "robotic" for you? Do you recognize whether fear or love is motivating what you are doing?

_____

_____

_____

_____

_____

_____

_____

INTERACTING WITH GOD

One thing that we can understand about friendship with God from our human relationships is that *friends love to be together*, and will shift their priorities and plans in order to do so. We also know that our friendships suffer if we are separated for long periods. We see this attitude in Moses:

Moses proves his friendship with God when he said, "If you're not going to the Promised Land, I am not going either!" Moses was saying to God, "You are more important to me than any vision that I have for my life." This is a key to building a deeper relationship with the Father. We must want Him more than we want what He does (Vallotton, 90).

Now, Scripture tells us that Moses was one of the very few people in the Old Testament who had personal access to the presence of God and saw His glory. It is no mistake that the man who had these encounters with God was so jealous to be with Him. The same passion was expressed by David hundreds of years later:

One thing I have desired of the Lord, that will I seek: that I may dwell in the house of the Lord all the days of my life, to behold the beauty of the Lord, and to inquire in His temple (Psalm 27:4).

Think about it: David and Moses were both leaders responsible for governing an entire nation of people. It's not as though they didn't bring their concerns to God in order to receive His wisdom and help. But this overwhelming desire simply to be with God reveals that their relationship went far beyond the professional level. One of the biggest things it indicates is that through their encounters with God they had a revelation that God wanted to be with them!

The common perception of God as Someone who only cares about people doing what He tells them to do and doing it right, is a result of sin separating us from God. God is not worried about getting stuff done. He is the most capable Person in existence. He doesn't need servants or slaves. The whole existence of the universe He created expresses His desire for family. So we should not think that He values individual tasks above the thing that, for Him, gives them their purpose and energy—and that is intimacy.

❧ Does your lifestyle reflect the priority of encountering the presence of God on a regular basis? If so, how does your intimacy with God affect your perception of the various tasks in your life? If not, what would you say is the top priority in your life?

_____

_____

_____

_____

_____

_____

❧ Do you feel like you are someone who can put tasks above relationships, both with God and with people? If so, might this be connected to a perception of God as being primarily task-oriented?

_____

_____

_____

_____

_____

_____

CONCLUSION

John the Apostle, who laid his head on the breast of Christ, had incredible insight into the heart of God. Here he finds the courage to record the following words that came from the mouth of Jesus himself, "If you abide in Me, and My words abide in you, ask whatever you wish, and it will be done for you" (John 15:7 NASB). Notice how being in right relationship with God gives us permission to ask for whatever we wish. The Bible is full of verses like this one. We are so accustomed to viewing the Scriptures through a slave's mentality that it seldom dawns on us that God actually likes the fact that we have a will. It was His idea to give us a brain (Vallotton, 93).

Invite the Holy Spirit to lead you into a deeper revelation of His desire for you to come to know Him as a friend and to become His friend. Spend some time imagining what it would be like to know God, love Him, and interact with Him like you do with your best friends. Ask Him to give you greater insight on what it means to abide in Him and for His words to abide in you. How would your relationship with God change if the main point was to be together, enjoy each other, and do life together? How would it change if you were fully confident that you had permission to ask God for anything you wished?

Chapter 8

SUPERHEROES IN THE SANCTUARY

BEING CHILDLIKE

When we were children we wanted to be someone special, but unfortunately the church has a way of beating that out of us by legalism and performance. We can do nothing to earn our Father's love. By simply "being" ourselves, we are precious and already glorious in His sight.

We need to get back to childlikeness in order to understand how exceptional we are to Him. Children who are being brought up in a healthy home know that their parents adore them and would do anything to protect them. They can do nothing to earn their parent's love because their parents loved them before they were conceived, just as our Father loved us before we could even know how to love Him: "We love Him because He first loved us" (1 John 4:19). We were wonderfully made from the beginning; it is part of our divine nature! (Vallotton, 99)

 HERE'S an interesting dynamic expressed here. On the one hand, we can look at children from healthy homes and learn something about the love of our heavenly Father for us. On the other hand, it is only the revelation of the love of our Father that will help us understand what true childlikeness is. This is also the revelation that will restore the holy desire for greatness in our hearts, for it is the love of parents that instills faith and value in the hearts of children and inspires them to become all that they can become.

Sadly, legalism and performance are not the only things that have the power to crush the heart of a child. Abuse or lack of love in the home can destroy a child's sense of value and desire for greatness. But the Cross has made a way for us to be fully restored to the people God made us to be when He created us. This is one of the biggest truths that we must come to believe if we are to leave pauperhood behind. It can feel like your poor choices or the poor choices of others have the power to keep you from your destiny. But that is a lie. God has filled His word with promises and testimonies that the redemption He accomplished through Christ is complete and has the power to transform you in this life and through eternity—not only to restore you to the innocence of a child, but to develop you into a mature son or daughter who looks just like Christ!

🕮 What is one promise you have received from God that shows His redemption is more powerful than anything else in your life? How has His love reawakened dreams and desires in your heart and inspired you to pursue your potential?

_____

_____

_____

The revelation of the love of God is what restores us to childlikeness by giving us our purpose, identity, and value. This is why Paul said the following:

> I bow my knees to the Father of our Lord Jesus Christ, from whom the whole family in heaven and earth is named, that He would grant you, according to the riches of His glory, to be strengthened with might through His Spirit in the inner man, that Christ may dwell in your hearts through faith; that you, being rooted and grounded in love, may be able to comprehend with all the saints what is the width and length and depth and height—to know the love of Christ which passes knowledge; that you may be filled with all the fullness of God (Ephesians 3:14-19).

This is simply an amazing prayer, and it models an important aspect of childlikeness for us. If we are lacking the revelation of the love of God in our lives, then all we need to do is ask our Father to give us the power to know His love! Jesus explained that *asking, seeking, and knocking* are some of the defining characteristics of childlikeness when He was teaching His disciples to pray:

> So I say to you, ask, and it will be given to you; seek, and you will find; knock, and it will be opened to you. If a son asks for bread from any father among you, will he give him a stone? Of if he asks for a fish, will he give him a serpent instead of a fish? Or if he asks for an egg, will he offer him a scorpion? If you then, being evil, know

how to give good gifts to your children, how much more will your heavenly Father give the Holy Spirit to those who ask Him! (Luke 11:9,11-13)

Before these verses, Jesus taught His disciples the Lord's Prayer, which includes the phrase, "Give us day by day our daily *bread*" (Luke 11:3). Then he told a story about asking your neighbor for *bread* and how your persistence will bring results. Then He said that fathers give *bread* to their children when they ask. The first point we can draw from this is that children of God are those who ask Him for what they need. But what does Jesus say that they receive from God? What is the true bread that will satisfy us? It's the same thing that Paul asked for to strengthen us in our inner beings to know the love of God—the Holy Spirit. When God answers our prayers, He doesn't just give us the thing we asked for. He gives us Himself. He doesn't want us merely to survive on the planet, but to thrive in every dimension of life. This is why true children of God aren't those who simply ask God to *do things for them*, but to *be with them*. Being in the presence of our Father and interacting with Him is what meets our deepest needs and desires as His children.

Of course, one of the difficulties we face in becoming those who ask, seek, and knock is that many of our experiences growing up train us not to do so. Most of us had parents or authority figures who neglected our needs, broke our trust in some way, or told us that the goal of adulthood was to be self-sufficient, independent, and proud of it. Asking, seeking, and knocking require us to acknowledge vulnerable areas of need and desire in our lives. This is why Jesus said:

Assuredly, I say to you, unless you are converted and become as little children, you will by no means enter the kingdom of heaven. Therefore whoever humbles himself as this little child is the greatest in the kingdom of heaven (Matthew 18:3-4).

❧ Do you have a hard time asking, seeking, and knocking? Do you recognize areas in your life where you want to be or feel you ought to be self-sufficient?

_____

_____

_____

❧ What does it look like to be a person who asks, seeks, and knocks as Christ taught and a person whose interactions with God aren't just focused on bringing a list of needs to Him?

_____

_____

_____

TRUSTING WHAT THE FATHER SAYS

Being childlike enough to ask, seek, and knock not only requires the humility to recognize your needs, but also to *trust* that the Father is good and will answer your requests. This heart of trust is expressed in another way: a child of God believes what the Father says about him or her. Consider:

Romans 8:28 is popular to quote when we are in trouble or having a bad day. It says, "We know that God causes all things to work together for good to those who love God, to those who are called according to His purpose" (NASB). What most of us have not understood is why all things work together for good. Look at the next two verses:

For those He foreknew, He also predestined to become conformed to the image of His Son, so that He would be the Firstborn among many brethren; and these whom He predestined, He also called; and these whom He called, He also justified; and these whom He justified, He also glorified (Romans 8:29-30).

Those He "foreknew" he also predestined for glory. God has already gone into our future and worked out all the circumstances so that we can become more glorious! That's why all things work together for good, because God created us with the end in mind. God starts from the end and works backward. He has looked at the finished product of His finest creation and said, "You are awesome!" (Vallotton, 101)

As we see here, understanding how God relates to time changes how we hear His promises to us. The cool thing is that when we learn to listen to His eternal perspective on our lives—the fact that everything is working together for our good—then we can learn to live outside of time. It doesn't mean we deny it when we are facing difficult circumstances, but that we deny the earthly, temporal version of what those circumstances mean when they disagree with God's version. We become more childlike as we accept the fact that our Father sees and knows things we simply can't see or understand yet, and trust His perspective above our own.

So, from God's perspective we are His children, and His whole plan for all of His kids is for us to end up looking just like our Elder Brother, Jesus Christ—which has many huge implications. But here is one issue it raises. Obviously God wanted us to know that He is working everything together for our good to make us more like Christ. The reason for letting us in on that fact is that He is not doing it in spite of us—He is doing it *with* us. He does everything through partnership. And we are better able to partner with Him when we understand what He is up to, because we learn to look for something particular no matter what our circumstances, and that is the revelation of Jesus and how we can become more like Him. It establishes a priority in our heart of getting to know our Elder Brother.

When you look at the life of Christ, what are some of the attitudes and behaviors that you wish most to emulate? Are there aspects of your Elder Brother that you have struggled to believe you could ever imitate? In what areas of your life does your Father's promise to make you like Christ need to be more firmly established?

_____

_____

_____

_____

_____

_____

MADE FOR GLORY

We were created for glory. Before the foundations of the earth we were made and predestined for greatness because He already knew we would choose Him. He set up our lives in such a way that we could not help but be awesome. You now have a right to believe you are indescribably irresistible just the way you were made! By choosing us first, He gave us the inheritance of greatness, for we are commissioned to be like Him, and He is glorious! (Vallotton, 102)

This last statement is the key to understanding how returning to childlikeness is connected to the restoration of a holy desire for greatness in our hearts: We are commissioned to be like him. Every child who grows up in a healthy family desires to be like his parents and to please them. C.S. Lewis described this truth thus:

When I began to look into this matter (of glory) I was shocked to find such different Christians as Milton, Johnson, and Thomas Aquinas taking heavenly glory quite frankly in the sense of fame or good report. But not fame conferred by our fellow creatures—fame with God, approval or (I might say) "appreciation" by God. And then...I suddenly remembered that no one can enter heaven except as a child; and nothing is so obvious in a child—not in a conceited child, but a good child—as its great and undisguised pleasure in being praised. Not only in a child, either, but even in a dog or a horse. Apparently what I had mistaken for humility had, all these years, prevented me from understanding what is in fact the humblest, the most childlike, the most creaturely of pleasures—nay, the specific pleasure of the inferior: the pleasure of a beast before men, a child before its father, a pupil before his teacher, a creature before its Creator.[1]

As children of God, our deepest desire is to please Him. The promise that God has and will glorify us shows us exactly where this desire came from and that God intends to fulfill it. In fact, the whole purpose of the New Covenant we've been brought into is to transform us with ever increasing measures of glory:

But we all, with unveiled face, beholding as in a mirror the glory of the Lord, are being transformed into the same image from glory to glory, just as by the Spirit of the Lord (2 Corinthians 3:18).

Notice that the way we become glorious is to behold the glory of the Lord. We were made to delight in God's presence as He delights in us, and it is simply being who He created us to be that allows the glory He has given us to shine out and glorify Him.

🔖 Do you struggle to believe that you are pleasing to God just the way you are? Do you "believe you are indescribably irresistible" to Him? What obstacles, if any, do you recognize in your heart or thinking that keep you from receiving God's delight and approval in your life?

_____

_____

_____

_____

_____

_____

_____

CONCLUSION

Invite the Holy Spirit to expose any areas in your life where He desires you to grow in the humility, trust, and delight of childlikeness. If you are worried about anything in your life, confess it to God and allow Him to bring His perfect peace and perspective into your circumstances. Meditate on the fact that He is working everything together for good.

ENDNOTE

1. C.S. Lewis, *The Weight of Glory*, (New York, NY: Harper-Collins, 1980), 36-37.

Chapter 9

ALL THE WAY DOWN TO THE TOP

EXALTING OUR GOD

The price that Jesus paid on the Cross determined the value of the people He purchased. We were created to share God's glory and bring Him glory. After all, who is greater—a king over a bunch of bozos, or a king over a great army of confident soldiers who take pride in serving their king? Isn't it true that the greatness of the King's subjects actually glorifies the King himself? (Vallotton, 104-5)

**P**ERHAPS the most notorious example in the Bible of a king who was glorified by his army of confident soldiers is David and his mighty men. These men followed David before he became king, and Scripture records that at the beginning these men were far from mighty at all:

Everyone who was in distress, everyone who was in debt, and everyone who was discontented gathered to him. So he became captain over them. And there were about four hundred men with him (1 Samuel 22:2).

But David was a mighty man himself, and a true leader. He raised up these men to be like him, and in the end, 37 of these men became so great that the Bible takes the trouble to record each of their names and in most cases, a sample of their exploits (see 2 Sam. 23:8-39).

In the New Testament, this scenario was repeated with Jesus and His disciples. When these men first came to Jesus, they were simple workmen with limited spiritual training. Under Jesus, they turned the world upside down (see Acts 17:6). He trained them to do everything He Himself did and promised them that their works would be greater than His.

In the case of both David and Jesus, we see leaders who raised their followers to be great and were not threatened by the idea that their followers' exploits could outstrip theirs. And we see in the cases of their followers that their loyalty to their leader was unshakable. It is significant that both groups were known by the name of their leader and didn't even think about trying to make their own names great. They were so impressed by the greatness of their kings that it probably would have struck them as ridiculous to aggrandize themselves.

Consider:

> The point is that as long as we acknowledge where our greatness comes from, we're not in danger of pride. We don't glorify God by saying we're not great, we glorify Him by acknowledging that He is the source of that greatness. Humility is not demeaning ourselves but exalting our God (Vallotton, 106).

What does exalting the Lord look like? Look at David's following statement:

> *My soul shall make its boast in the Lord; the humble shall hear of it and be glad* (Psalm 34:2).

✍ Boasting can actually be an expression of true humility! The issue is what we are boasting *in*. Do you make it a regular practice to boast in the Lord—to praise, thank and worship Him, and declare His greatness? How important would you say this practice is in helping you keep your focus on Him and what He's doing as opposed to on yourself?

_____

_____

_____

Worship—exalting God—is the key to humility, because it is in worship that we see God for who He truly is and ourselves for who we truly are:

> The only way we can be truly humble is to have an honest assessment of ourselves before God (Vallotton, 106).

When Paul described the fall of man to the Romans, he declared:

*For since the creation of the world His invisible attributes are clearly seen, being understood by the things that are made, even His eternal power and Godhead, so that they are without excuse, because, **although they knew God, they did not glorify Him as God, nor were thankful,** but became futile in their thoughts, and their foolish hearts were darkened* (Romans 1:20-21).

The corollary truth to the principle expressed in this verse is that glorifying God and giving Him thanks are keys to keeping our thoughts connected to our purpose and our hearts enlightened by the truth. So think about it. Have there been times in your life when you have lost your sense of purpose, or when short-term goals and tasks became more important than your calling? Were consistent worship and time with God lacking in these seasons? What part does worship play in helping you keep the truth of your identity, calling, and who God is active in your heart and mind?

RESTRAINING OUR STRENGTH

True humility is not the absence of confidence but strength restrained...Humility is an issue of the heart. We can't be humble by accident; we must purpose in our hearts to know our greatness yet never exalt ourselves higher than we ought...We can be people of humility and still be confident in who we are. Unfortunately, confidence always looks like arrogance to the insecure (Vallotton, 106).

We've already looked at the fact that Christ was the ultimate model of humility and servanthood. He restrained His strength by emptying Himself of His privileges as God and taking on the limitations of humanity. But the Gospels record that Jesus wasn't always perceived as a model of humility. Jesus regularly offended the Pharisees and even His own followers by making statements that struck them as arrogant and blasphemous. Here is a typical response to His statements:

> *Then the Jews took up stones again to stone Him. Jesus answered them, "Many good works I have shown you from My Father. For which of those works do you stone Me?" The Jews answered Him, saying, "For a good work we do not stone You, but for blasphemy, and because You, being a Man, make Yourself God"* (John 10:31-33).

The point is that *the perception of people really has nothing to do with whether a person is truly humble.* Humility is an issue of how you relate to God and how He perceives you. The reality is that it is a *byproduct* of understanding and believing the truth of who God is and who you are in Him. It is true that humility is a choice, but the fact is that the best way to choose humility is to choose to believe what God says about you. *Faith* is the primary trait we must cultivate in our lives in order to "purpose...to know our greatness." It is when we step out on the words we have heard from our Father that we truly discover what is inside of us and, consequently, are able to learn how to restrain our strength. Faith is the most humble attribute we can cultivate in our lives.

Why is it humble to believe what God says about you?

_____

_____

_____

_____

_____

_____

_____

The fact that Christ humbled Himself in becoming a man obviously did not mean that He never displayed great strength and boldness. So what does it mean to restrain your strength?

_____

_____

_____

_____

_____

_____

_____

THE PURPOSE OF GREATNESS

John the Baptist was a great example of humility. He was a great man, and Jesus Himself praised him and declared that he was the greatest of all men "born of women" (see Matt. 11:11)! He knew who he was and faithfully and boldly fulfilled his divine assignment to prepare the way for the Lord. But when Christ was revealed and began His ministry, John willingly stepped aside. He said, "He must increase, but I must decrease" (John 3:30). The question is, Was John putting himself down in this statement? The answer is that *he didn't need to*. He was simply stating a fact—when Jesus increases, everything else necessarily gets smaller. True humility comes from simply seeing ourselves in the right context.

So far we have been looking at seeing our greatness in the context of who God is. We also need to see our greatness in the context of its purpose:

> God has given the Church a great call, and therefore it takes great people to accomplish it. If we fail to see our greatness, we will fall short of our call. Our pauper mentality and false humility have rendered much of the Church ineffective by diminishing our vision for the influence we are meant to have in the world (Vallotton, 107).

We have all encountered people in the world around us who are arrogant and egotistical. Some of these people have achieved real greatness in some area of life through developing their talents with hard work and determination. The tragedy in these cases is not that these men and women are taking all the credit for what they've done; it's that their greatness hasn't been directed toward the divine purpose for which they were created. Can you imagine what our world would be like if every talent and ability given to humankind was directed toward the praise and glory of God? Then the knowledge of the glory of the Lord would truly cover the earth as the waters cover the sea (see Hab. 2:14)!

In the parable of the talents (see Matt. 25:14-30), the successful servants were those who understood that their master had entrusted them with some of his wealth to be *used* for the purpose of increasing it. This is what God desires us to understand about the greatness He has put in us. There won't be a question of us becoming proud when we truly understand and embrace the *responsibility* that comes with it. Instead, we will become sober-minded, disciplined, and passionate about developing what we've received in order to fulfill our calling.

   ❧ What are some of the primary talents and abilities that God has given you? What are some of the things that you love to do, or areas of life that you desire to be involved in? How are these areas connected to divine purpose in your life? Where do you feel the greatest level of responsibility in your life?

_____

_____

_____

_____

_____

_____

_____

Do you have a sense of the greatness of the call that God has put on your life as His son or daughter, or do you usually feel that you can't or shouldn't be a great person? Do you recognize where a pauper mentality has diminished your vision for influencing the world?

_____

_____

_____

_____

_____

_____

_____

REVEALING HIS ROYALTY

The apostle John said, "As He is, (speaking of Jesus) so also are we in this world" (1 John 4:17). Notice he didn't say, "As He was", but instead he said, "As He is." Jesus is not the suffering servant carrying His Cross anymore. He is the coming King. We are to be the revelation of His royalty on the earth...The full revelation of what it means to be saved still needs to penetrate our thinking until we understand that who we were is totally dead and who we are is the revelation of Christ on the earth. When we came to Christ, it was humility to honestly assess ourselves as sinners. To go back and say that's still who we are is to deny what Christ did for us. Doing that is no longer humbling ourselves, it's undercutting the resurrection power God has given us to live like Him (Vallotton, 108-109).

Let's consider the aspect of being saved that is perhaps most central in Paul's teaching on salvation:

There is therefore now no condemnation to those who are in Christ Jesus, who do not walk according to the flesh, but according to the Spirit. For the law of the Spirit of life in Christ Jesus has made me free from the law of sin and death...And if Christ is in you, the body is dead because of sin, but the Spirit is life because of righteousness. But if the Spirit of Him who raised Jesus from the dead dwells in you, He who raised Christ from the dead will also give life to your mortal bodies through His Spirit who dwells in you (Romans 8:1-2,10-11).

Paul repeatedly outlines two modes of human existence. One mode is defined by the flesh, sin, death, and the law; the other mode is defined by the resurrection life and freedom that the Spirit of God brings into the spirits and bodies of those He indwells. There is no possibility in Paul's mind of a life in the Spirit that still features any of the old limitations of life under the law of sin and death. Instead, life in the Spirit leads directly to the following:

For as many as are led by the Spirit of God, these are the sons of God...The Spirit Himself bears witness with our spirit that we are children of God, and if children, then heirs—heirs of God and joint heirs with Christ, if indeed we suffer with Him, that we may also be glorified together. For I consider that the sufferings of this present time are not worthy to be compared with the glory which shall be revealed in us. For the earnest expectation of the creation eagerly waits for the revealing of the sons of God (Romans 8:14,16-19).

Life as the sons and daughters of the King, life in the Spirit, is intended to culminate in a global unveiling of the glory of God on His family. Why does creation wait for this unveiling? The next verses declare:

For the creation was subjected to futility, not willingly, but because of Him who subjected it in hope; because the creation itself also will be delivered from the bondage of corruption into the glorious liberty of the children of God (Romans 8:20-21).

The revelation of the glory of God in us is directly tied to the restoration of all creation to its original purpose. That is the hope of Heaven. That is how high the stakes have been raised.

So the fact that we could undercut the flow of resurrection life through us by effectively denying the work of the Cross and holding on to our old identities is not a matter to be taken lightly. In fact, it is precisely what our enemy would like us to do.

&- Paul lays down the defining characteristic of a son or daughter of God—the characteristic that enables a person to become a revelation of Jesus on the earth. God's children are *led by His Spirit*. What would you say are some of the primary attributes of a person who is led by the Spirit?

&- Look at the context of the verse referred to above: "Love has been perfected among us in this: that we may have boldness in the day of judgment; because as He is, so are we in this world. There is no fear in love..." (1 John 4:17-18). One of the primary ways that we reveal the risen Christ is when our lives display a conspicuous lack of fear and the strong presence of bold love. Do you recognize if and where you deal with issues of fear in your life? How are these areas holding you back from your calling to display Christ?

CONCLUSION

God never reminds us of our smallness when He calls us to do something awesome. Instead he calls us to courage by proclaiming something amazing over us like, "You're a mighty warrior," "A father of many nations," or "You're the one that all of Israel is waiting on!" (Vallotton, 109)

Invite the Holy Spirit to remind you of who you are today and what He has called you to do. Renew your commitment to walk in sonship by following His lead and believing what He says. Ask Him to unveil any areas where insecurity and false humility have been holding you back from developing and displaying the greatness He has put in you in order to fulfill your high calling.

Chapter 10

HONOR—
THE YELLOW BRICK ROAD

LOVE OTHERS AS YOU LOVE YOURSELF

Honor is humility in action. It is a matter of the heart and requires an honest assessment of the value of other people and a choice to focus on that above ourselves. As a friend of mine stated, "Arrogance isn't thinking too much of ourselves but thinking too little of others" (Vallotton, 123).

ONE of the words translated "honor" in the New Testament is the Greek word *timao*, which means, "to estimate, to fix the value."[1] How do we fix the value on other people? Well, God tells us repeatedly throughout the Bible to be fair and value others according to the value we place on ourselves, or, as He puts it most often, to love one another as we love ourselves:

Do not seek revenge or bear a grudge against one of your people, **but love your neighbor as yourself***...The stranger who dwells among you shall be to you as one born among you, and* **you shall love him as yourself;** *for you were strangers in the land of Egypt...*(Leviticus 19:18 NIV, 34 NKJV).

You shall **love your neighbor as yourself** (Mark 12:31).

It is interesting that the assumption implicit in these statements is that loving oneself is something that everyone at some level knows about. There aren't many passages of Scripture devoted specifically to teaching people how to love themselves. We are commanded, by default, to love ourselves in these passages—for otherwise we could not fulfill the command to love our neighbors as ourselves—but a direct command or exhortation to love ourselves is hard to find in Scripture. Yet we've been spending a significant portion of this study endeavoring to value and love ourselves in the right way—in the way that God values us. The command to love our neighbors as we love ourselves does not preclude the fact that we are going to need to learn how to do both on some level.

If we must learn to love both ourselves and others, why is it that the Bible focuses primarily on the second task? Consider the implications of a statement made by Paul on the topic of husbands loving their wives. He says:

> So husbands ought to love their own wives as their own bodies; **he who loves his wife loves himself.** After all, no one ever hated his own flesh, but nourishes and cherishes it (Ephesians 5:28-29).

It turns out that, at least when it comes to husbands loving their wives, *the way to love yourself is to love your wife.* The big question is, Does this principle apply to loving our neighbors, strangers, and even our enemies as well? Could the truth behind the command to love others as ourselves be that loving others is in fact one of the primary ways that we truly love ourselves? There is a very good chance that it is. Certainly, husbands and wives have a covenant relationship and have become one flesh, and in such a relationship, it is easy to understand how loving one another is beneficial to both parties. However, when Paul tells husbands to love their wives, he explains that this love they are to show is the same love that Christ showed to the Church. Christ repeatedly commanded us to love one another as He loved us, and explained that we have become members of one another in His body. We are joined to Christ and to one another with the same covenant obligation to love one another unconditionally as marriage partners have. The principle for husbands thus applies to the rest of us as well.

   In your experience and knowledge, would you say that loving others is a way to love yourself? Why or why not? How have you seen this truth play out in your life?

_____

_____

_____

How is this principle similar to Christ's statement, "For whoever desires to save his life will lose it, but whoever loses his life for My sake will find it" (Matt. 16:25)?

As we learn to value ourselves in the right way, one of the things we discover is that valuing others is part of that process. The interesting thing is that most of the truths that make us valuable in God's eyes are truths common to every believer—even to every person. We read in the last chapter that, "The price that Jesus paid on the Cross determined the value of the people He purchased" (Vallotton, 104). We know that Christ died for the whole world. The price that He paid for each person was the same, and therefore, the value of each person is the same. Thus, the truths by which we come to value ourselves are the same truths that guide us to value one another. These reasons are precisely why we *can* and *should* make "an honest assessment of the value of other people and a choice to focus on that above ourselves."

⚜ What are some of the other things that make you valuable? Are these things also true of other people? What are some of the reasons that God wants us to make a conscious choice to focus on the value of others above ourselves?

_____

_____

_____

_____

_____

CARRYING A STANDARD

At its foundation, honor flows from the conviction that people are extremely valuable, and that this value all flows directly from *God's actions*, not human actions. This conviction is the key to becoming an *honorable person*:

> Whenever we treat people honorably even if they refuse to honor us, we demonstrate that we have a standard within us that isn't determined by the people around us. We don't just honor people because they are honorable, but we honor people because we are honorable. For a Christian, honor is a condition of the heart, not just the product of a good environment. Honor doesn't mean we agree with the people we are honoring; it simply means we value them as people who have been created in the image and likeness of God (Vallotton, 118).

The issue of honoring those who dishonor us or disagree with us can be a tough one. We face the same problem in fulfilling Jesus' command to love our enemies. Consider the reason Jesus gives us for doing this:

*You have heard that it was said, "You shall love your neighbor and hate your enemy." But I say to you, love your enemies, bless those who curse you, do good to those who hate you, and pray for those who spitefully use you and persecute you, **that you may be sons of your Father in heaven; for He makes His sun rise on the evil and on the good and sends rain on the just and on the unjust.** For if you love those who love you, what reward have you? Do not even the tax collectors do the same? And if you greet your brethren only, what do you do more than others? Do not even the tax collectors do so? Therefore, **you shall be perfect, just as your Father in heaven is perfect** (Matthew 5:43-48).*

The word translated *perfect* here also means "wanting nothing necessary to completeness" and "mature."[2] Maturity in the sons of God is seen in the fact that they show the same love to those who mistreat, hate and abuse them as to those who love them—just like God does.

The command to be perfect, like the command to heal the sick or raise the dead, is something that is usually difficult for most of us to wrap our minds and hearts around. This is where we need the willing heart of a friend that trusts the heart of Jesus, a heart that says, "If He said it, it must be possible, and He must be willing to help me do it. He isn't setting me up to fail. He isn't exposing my flaws in order to show me how far I fall short and leave me where I am. He's just showing me what a true prince or princess acts like so I can grow up into that."

  Jesus said the treatment we're to give to all people, including the dishonorable, is to love them, *bless* them, *do good* to them, and *pray* for them. Is there a person in your life who has treated you dishonorably, or with whom you disagree on things? Are you treating that individual the way Jesus has taught? How would you change if you saw your relationship with this person as an opportunity for the royal nature of Christ in you to be expressed?

_____

_____

_____

LOVE CASTS OUT FEAR

Romans 12:10 instructs us, "Be kindly affectionate to one another with brotherly *love*, in *honor* giving preference to one another" (Rom. 12:10). Honor is love in action as well as humility in action. And First John 4:18 tells us that when the "perfect" love that Jesus described in Matthew 5 is expressed, one of the main things that happens is that fear goes away:

There is no fear in love. But perfect love drives out fear, because fear has to do with punishment. The one who fears is not made perfect in love (1 John 4:18 NIV).

Since honor is an expression of perfect love, it has the same effect:

Honor is the cornerstone of an empowering culture that eliminates the need for control. The presence of honor creates order through dignity instead of the fear of punishment. Order, when it is fostered by honor, results in empowerment; order enforced through fear results in control. If we were to take negative consequences out of an environment where the people don't have honor in their hearts for one another, disorder and chaos would surely develop. People either obey their leaders because they are afraid of what might happen if they don't, or they do what is asked of them because they have honor in their hearts and respect those who have authority over them (Vallotton, 119).

  ❧ What are some of the main characteristics of an environment, whether it is a home, a church, or a community, that is ordered by control? What are some of the things that are prevented from happening when people are controlled through the fear of punishment?

_____

_____

_____

_____

What are some of the main characteristics of an environment in which people are empowered? What are some of the things that can be expressed in a place of freedom, and why is it safe to do so?

_____

_____

_____

_____

In particular, how does a controlling environment respond to people's sin or mistakes and how is it different than the response in an empowering environment? What are the consequences of either result?

_____

_____

_____

_____

HONORING THOSE IN AUTHORITY

While the Bible teaches us to honor everyone, it specifically teaches us to give special honor to the following people:

Honor your father and your mother (Matthew 19:19).

Let the elders who rule well be counted worthy of double honor, especially those who labor in the word and doctrine (1 Timothy 5:17).

Honor the king (1 Peter 2:17).

Once again, the heart attitude of honor is connected to the value we have for people. So what is it that makes parents, elders, and leaders valuable? Consider:

> God often describes people with the words "least" and "greatest". The government of Heaven is like a rectangular table. With this structure, we recognize that there are people who have been elevated above others and that they have something we need. Just as Elisha recognized that he needed Elijah's mantle, so we have much to receive from those who have gone beyond us. In order to receive an inheritance and impartation from them, we need to have faith and expectation that they truly do have much to give. We show this by honoring them. Life flows from honoring them in our hearts (Vallotton, 123).

Why does it take faith to honor people in authority? Well, you'll notice that in two of the three cases above, the Bible doesn't say to give this special honor only to the people that we deem worthy. There may be kings, parents, and leaders whom we disagree with or flat out don't like, but we are still to give them honor. King David is probably the most shining example of someone who showed honor to an unworthy leader, King Saul. Even in situations where it looked like God was setting him up to get rid of Saul and take his rightful place on the throne, David declared:

> *The Lord forbid that I should do this thing to my master, the Lord's anointed, to stretch out my hand against him, seeing he is the anointed of the Lord* (1 Samuel 24:6).

Like David, the thing in which we can put our faith and expectation is not any particular person, but the authority structure that God has built into our families, the Church, and society. Paul declared:

> *Let every soul be subject to the governing authorities. For there is no authority except from God, and the authorities that exist are appointed by God* (Romans 13:1).

When we honor those who hold positions of authority, in any and every sphere of life, we come into agreement with what God has done in appointing them. These people may be poor stewards of the authority they've been given, but surely our job is not to judge them or defame them. Instead, the fact that we've been commanded to honor them means that we must be intentional in making them the target of the kinds of acts of love Jesus prescribed: blessing them, doing good to them, and praying for them. Our desire should be for them to discover the true source and responsibility of their authority so they can cooperate with Heaven.

Every time we come into agreement with what God is doing, we allow the grace and power of the Kingdom to flow in and through our lives. This is the reason that life flows through honor—it is an agreement with God.

God does tell us that when we are faithful to honor our parents, He will be faithful to His promise to give us long life. What are some of the aspects of "life"—the blessings, whether material or spiritual—that have flowed to you through obedience to this command?

_____

_____

_____

_____

When you see someone who is walking ahead of you in some area of life, particularly in an area where you desire to excel, how does it affect you? Do you see him or her as someone from whom you could inherit wisdom and encouragement, or do you feel intimidated by that person? What would it look like to honor that person?

_____

_____

_____

_____

CONCLUSION

In Esther 6 we read of an interesting story. One night, the king couldn't sleep, so he started to read through the royal records. Eventually he came upon an entry declaring that Mordecai the Jew had thwarted a plot to assassinate him. What bothered him was that nothing had been done to honor Mordecai for his service. In a perfect act of poetic, divine justice, the plan he adopted to honor the man who saved his life led to the humiliation of the man who was plotting to kill the Jews, Haman. It is a wonderful picture of how honor in action releases the justice and order of Heaven.

Invite the Holy Spirit to reveal people in your life who deserve specific acts of honor, whether it be for the reason that they are made in the image of God, that they are in a position of authority, or that, like Mordecai, they have done something that deserves to be recognized. Then ask Him to show you the practical steps to show honor to them.

ENDNOTES

1. Strong's Greek, accessed May 2008, taken from http://cf.blueletterbible.org/lang/lexicon/lexicon.cfm? Strongs=G5406&t=KJV; s.v. "*timao*."

2. Strong's Greek, accessed May 2008, taken from http://cf.blueletterbible.org/lang/lexicon/lexicon.cfm? Strongs=G5046&t=KJV; s.v. "perfect."

Chapter 11

ROYALTY IS DYING TO BE TOGETHER

BECOMING A FAMILY

When the Church of Jesus becomes a family instead of a harem, people won't just come to church, they will become the church. It will no longer be a place they go to but a tribe they live in, a people they have responsibility for and a family that nurtures one another in good times and in bad, in sickness and health, until death do us part. They won't change churches just because the worship isn't as good as Joe's Super Church down the street. They will be committed to a family where they hear the voice of their Shepherd in the people who are leading them (Vallotton, 131).

ow does the Church of God become a family? We know that we have been called sons and daughters of God in Christ, and are therefore brothers and sisters. But what characterizes the relationships that God desires for us to have with one another, and what is necessary for us to develop these characteristics?

Let us first consider the characteristics of the relationships God desires us to have as believers. When Jesus prepared to leave His disciples and go to the Cross, He said:

By this all will know that you are My disciples, if you have love for one another...This is My commandment, that you love one another as I have loved you (John 13:35; 15:12).

Christ's love is to define our relationships with one another. How did Jesus love us? In one of the most famous passages of Scripture, Paul describes the nature of Christ-like, perfect love:

Love never gives up. Love cares more for others than for self. Love doesn't want what it doesn't have. Love doesn't strut, doesn't have a swelled head, doesn't force itself on others, isn't always "me first," doesn't fly off the handle, doesn't keep score of the sins of others, doesn't revel when others grovel, takes pleasure in the flowering of truth, puts up with anything, trusts God always, always looks for the best, never looks back, but keeps going to the end. Love never dies (1 Corinthians 13:4-8, The Message).

❧ Love never gives up, keeps going to the end, and never dies. What are some words that you might use to describe these aspects of love? How well would you say that these qualities characterize your relationships with your brothers and sisters in Christ?

_____

_____

_____

Let's consider one of the Bible's prescriptions for developing Christ's love in our lives. As we have seen, our royal identity and royal behavior all flow from walking in submission to the Spirit and allowing His power to flow through our lives, as Paul declared: "For as many as are led by the Spirit of God, these are the sons of God" (Rom. 8:14). In his letter to the Galatians, Paul explains that being led by the Spirit is directly antithetical to living for self, and describes the differences between a Spirit-led and a selfish lifestyle:

My counsel is this: Live freely, animated and motivated by God's Spirit. Then you won't feed the compulsions of selfishness. For there is a root of sinful self-interest in us that is at odds with a free spirit, just as the free spirit is incompatible with selfishness...It is obvious what kind of life develops out of trying to get your own way all the time: repetitive, loveless, cheap sex; a stinking accumulation of mental and emotional garbage; frenzied and joyless grabs for happiness; trinket gods; magic-show religion; paranoid loneliness; cutthroat competition; all-consuming-yet-never-satisfied wants; a brutal temper; **an impotence to love or be loved; divided homes and divided lives;** *small-minded and lopsided pursuits; the vicious habit of depersonalizing everyone into a rival; uncontrolled and uncontrollable addictions;* **ugly parodies of community.** *I could go on....*

*But what happens when we live God's way? He brings gifts into our lives, much the same way that fruit appears in an orchard—things like **affection for others,** exuberance about life, serenity. **We develop a willingness to stick with things,** a sense of compassion in the heart, and a conviction that a basic holiness permeates things and people. We find ourselves involved in **loyal commitments,** not needing to force our way in life, able to marshal and direct our energies wisely* (Galatians 5:16-17,19-21, 22-23 The Message).

Here we see two diametrically opposed sources for the two types of relationships and communities explored in this chapter. One type is characterized by division, unfaithfulness, lack of love, competition, and a focus on getting one's needs met; it all flows from selfishness. The other type is characterized by affection, loyalty, perseverance, generosity, and commitment, and it flows from the Spirit. The thing to notice is that Paul insists that it is our responsibility to choose which source we are going to draw from:

It is absolutely clear that God has called you to a free life. Just make sure that you don't use this freedom as an excuse to do whatever you want to do and destroy your freedom. Rather, use your freedom to serve one another in love; that's how freedom grows. For everything we know about God's Word is summed up in a single sentence: Love others as you love yourself. That's an act of true freedom. If you bite and ravage each other, watch out—in no time at all you will be annihilating each other, and where will your precious freedom be then? (Galatians 5:13-15 The Message)

❧ What are some of the areas of your daily life that present you with the choice to follow the lead of the Spirit or give into selfishness? When you choose to be led by the Spirit in these areas, what is the result? When you choose to be led by selfishness, what is the result?

_____

_____

_____

🙠 Which of the fruits of the Spirit mentioned above do you see in your life? Which ones do you desire to see more of? If these things are *fruits*, that is, the consequences of following the Spirit, then what is the key to bearing more of them in your life?

_____

_____

_____

_____

_____

_____

THE NATURE OF OUR COVENANT

Almost 3,000 years ago, the prophet Malachi knew the importance of reuniting fathers and sons in the last days. He saw the restoration of covenant relationships as the force that would shatter the curses of our land. This last days' revival will be founded in both the natural and spiritual family. Curses are the powerful and the painful cost of absent and broken covenants (Vallotton, 132).

Along with prophesying about the restoration of fathers and sons, Malachi also addressed the issue of the covenant between husband and wife, particularly what it meant to break that covenant through divorce:

> **Did He not make them one,** having a remnant of the Spirit? And why one? He seeks godly offspring. Therefore take heed to your spirit, and let none deal treacherously with the wife of his youth. For the Lord God of Israel says that He hates divorce, for it covers one's garment with violence (Malachi 2:15-16a).

God considers it an act of violence to separate two people who have become "one" in marriage. This act of violence cannot help but have serious consequences. For one thing, as God explains in the previous verses of this passage, divorce, unfaithfulness, and other violations of covenant cut you off from Him:

> *You cover the altar of the Lord with tears, with weeping and crying; so He does not regard the offering anymore, nor receive it with goodwill from your hands...Because the Lord has been witness between you and the wife of your youth, with whom you have dealt treacherously* (Malachi 2:13-14).

But is the covenant that we have been brought into in the Body of Christ like the covenant of marriage? Consider:

> *For as we have many members in **one** body, but all the members do not have the same function, so we, being many, are **one** body in Christ, and individually **members of one another*** (Romans 12:4-5).

Perhaps even a more powerful expression of our relationship as believers is expressed in Jesus' High Priestly prayer in John 17. He prayed:

> *I do not pray for these alone, but also for those who will believe in Me through their word; **that they all may be one,** as You, Father, are in Me, and I in You; that they also may be **one** in Us, that the world may believe that You sent Me. And the glory which You gave Me I have given them, that they may be **one** just as We are **one**: I in them, and You in Me; that they may be made perfect in **one**, and that the world may know that You have sent Me, and have loved them as You have loved Me* (John 17:20-23).

As we can see, Jesus uses the same word to describe our relationship with one another as God used to describe the covenant of marriage: we are *one*. And we have been made one by God Himself. When we violate that covenant in any way, we are standing in direct opposition to the will of God.

🙢 Have you witnessed or experienced the effects of broken covenants in your life, and if so, what are they? Have you witnessed or experienced restoration after a broken covenant, and if so, what were some of the key elements involved in this process?

_____

_____

_____

🙢 What does it mean to be "members of one another"? What are some of the implications of the fact that we have been made one through the Spirit of Christ? Why do you suppose that Christ cared so much about His body being one?

_____

_____

_____

🙢 How is the unity of the Body of Christ connected to the world knowing that Christ came from the Father?

_____

_____

_____

GENEROSITY

The focus of each member of (a) covenant is, "I'm in this relationship for what I can give to it, not just for what I can receive from it."...The mark of true royalty is the ability to lay down our lives in covenant with others for the sake of the kingdom (Vallotton, 134, 138).

Generosity, the posture of giving, is what characterizes the royal family of God. Significantly, this was one of the first traits expressed among the believers in the early church in Jerusalem:

> *Nor was there anyone among them who lacked; for all who were possessors of lands or houses sold them, and brought the proceeds of the things that were sold, and laid them at the apostles feet; and they distributed to each as anyone had need* (Acts 4:34-35).

There is something about the expression of God's generosity in the outpouring of His Spirit that moves us to respond to Him and others in the same way. When we get in touch with the limitlessness of our Father's Kingdom and the fact that He has given all of His sons and daughters access to it, it shifts our thinking and priorities so that we begin to show radical, sacrificial generosity. Likewise, when the revelation that God has withheld nothing from us truly penetrates our hearts, the only obvious response will be to do the same. Consider:

> *He who did not spare His own Son, but delivered Him up for us all, how shall He not with Him also freely give us **all things**?* (Romans 8:32)

> *For **all things** are yours: whether Paul or Apollos or Cephas, or the world or life or death, or things present or things to come—**all are yours*** (1 Corinthians 3:21-22).

God has withheld nothing from us. That's what our King does, and that is what His sons and daughters do. But true royal generosity, just like true love, humility, and honor, can only flow from the heart:

> *He who sows sparingly will also reap sparingly, and he who sows bountifully will also reap bountifully. So let each one give as he **purposes in his heart,** not grudgingly or of necessity; for God loves a **cheerful giver.** And God is able to make **all grace** abound toward you, that you, always having all sufficiency **in all things,** may have abundance for **every good work*** (2 Corinthians 9:6-8).

God has made *all grace* available to us. There is no holding back on His end. But our role as co-laborers is to receive this grace and make it available to others. Remember, we are "members of one another," and the process by which the Body of Christ grows to maturity involves "the whole body, joined and knit together by what every joint supplies, according to the effective working by which every part does its share" (Eph. 4:16). The covenant relationship we've been brought into is designed in such a way that everything we receive from God is actually meant to supply what is needed to the "joints" around you. When we are all fulfilling our role of giving, everyone benefits.

🌫 Why do you think that our attitude in giving is so important to God? What purposes does a cheerful giver establish in his or her heart?

_____

_____

_____

_____

🌫 Is getting your needs met driving your priorities in any of the following areas: finances, relationships, church, career, and health? How would you change if you knew that everything you needed was completely provided for?

_____

_____

_____

_____

CONCLUSION

Invite the Holy Spirit to speak to you about the "loyal commitments" that He has called you to walk in. Allow Him to expose any areas where you are focusing more on what you're getting from these relationships than what you are giving to them. God is a cheerful giver. Ask Him to expand the revelation of His generosity and to lead you into a more mature expression of His royal nature in you.

Chapter 12

DEFENDING THE DECREES OF THE KING

CLOSING THE DISTANCE

Gideon was tired of hiding in the winepress beating out wheat...He had been hearing the prophet's reminder of all Israel had seen God do, and he wanted to know why there was such a huge gap between the miraculous works of the past and Israel's utter powerlessness to change their present circumstances. Like us, he wanted to know why there was such a distance between what the Bible said there should be and what he was actually experiencing. Royalty cannot live with this incongruity in their hearts (Vallotton, 140-141).

✎ Have you noticed an incongruity between what people experienced under Jesus' ministry and what you and those around you experience? How has this incongruity affected you and how have you chosen to respond to it?

_____

_____

_____

_____

For many of us, the most disconcerting aspect of the incongruity between the Bible and our experience is not only that much of the Church still has a much lower success rate than Jesus, who healed, delivered, and forgave everyone without exception who came to Him for help. What bothers us, and should bother us, is the fact that Jesus made the following promise:

*Most assuredly, I say to you, he who believes in Me, the **works that I do** he will do also; and **greater works** than these he will do, because I go to My Father* (John 14:12)

Studied in its context, there is no possibility that Jesus can be referring to anything but the *miraculous works* that He had performed all throughout His ministry—the signs of His identity as the Messiah. Likewise, He said:

And these signs will follow those who believe: In My Name they will cast out demons; they will speak with new tongues; they will take up serpents; and if they drink anything deadly, it will by no means hurt them; they will lay hands on the sick, and they will recover (Mark 16:17-18).

You'll notice that in both of these statements, Jesus identifies those who will perform these works and signs as *believers*. We most often use that term to describe people who go to church, read their Bibles, and pray, but the life of the believer is to be marked by the supernatural works of Jesus. After all, the life of the believer begins with a miracle. As we have seen, the Spirit of resurrection brought us to life at our conversion. All of us experienced the superior reality of the Kingdom as it began to affect us, empowering us to leave our old habits, receive healing from the past, and be filled with peace and joy. It is only natural for those who have been raised from the dead and filled with the Spirit of God Himself to hunger for, and demonstrate the reality of, our Father's Kingdom. The Christian life is miraculous.

Jesus declared, "As the Father has sent me, I also send you" (John 20:21). We are the representatives of Christ in the same way that Christ represented the Father to us. Thus, it is our destiny as believers to close the gap between the reality of our Father's kingdom and the visible world around us. Everything that Jesus had available to Him is available to us. God has set us up for success in every area.

There are four things we must do if we are going to grow up into our destiny to walk in the supernatural. First, we need to be convinced that it is our destiny. Otherwise, we will hear the statement that those who believe in Christ will do greater works—like the statement that those who love Him obey His commands—as an impossible standard designed to expose just how far we fall short of being like Christ. Second, we must avoid developing a negative focus by looking at where we're not, who we're not, and what's not going on in our lives. Third, we must guard our hearts against disappointment and unbelief as we contend for breakthrough and experience confusing results. And last, we must feed our hearts and minds on the promises of God and renew our willingness to step out in faith and obedience in our daily lives.

🙤 Do you struggle with a negative focus in your life—with focusing on what you're not instead of who you are, or focusing on what God isn't doing rather than what He is doing? What impact is this focus having on your life?

_____

_____

_____

_____

🙤 Did you use to be more passionate about seeing the miraculous in your life than you are now? Would you say that this change is related to a lessening of expectation due to a lighter "diet" of feeding on the promises of God, or to embracing disappointment when you didn't see breakthrough?

_____

_____

_____

_____

A wrong focus, a failure to maintain a posture of faith through feeding on promises, and disappointment are all dealt with in the same way: repentance. In repentance, the harmful pattern is broken and grace is available to start fresh in pursuing your destiny.

BEING PROVOKED

Many in the Body of Christ are in the same state Saul was in before he encountered injustice. We have been anointed as kings and priests, we have been commanded to disciple nations, and we have been equipped with the wisdom, power and authority of God Himself. Yet somehow we find ourselves following some silly oxen around the farm, going back to our old habits and focusing on survival when we've been called to lead and influence people for the Kingdom. However, injustice has a way of drawing out the royal call in our lives. We can always tell how much of our princely identity we are truly walking in by our response to injustice: either our spirits get provoked within us, driving us to act, or we run for cover (Vallotton, 142).

Because it is our destiny to do the impossible, it should not surprise us when God calls us to do something outrageous, risky, and unheard of. Imagine what Saul must have felt like being called to such a powerful role in his nation, a role that had never even existed before. Imagine what Abraham must have felt like being called to leave his father's house to wander around in the desert until God brought him to the land of his destiny. Imagine what Mary felt like being asked to bear a child out of wedlock in the midst of a religious culture, where most people would probably have accused her of telling a blasphemous lie to cover her immorality. On this side of their decisions, of course, we see how crucial their obedience and faith in God turned out to be. But we do not always see the same truth when God presents us with the assignment He has for us.

Every God-assignment is connected to His will, expressed by Christ in the prayer, "Your Kingdom come. Your will be done on earth as it is in heaven" (Matt. 6:10). Whether it is leading a country or having a baby, a God-assignment is designed to release the reality of His Kingdom on earth as it is in Heaven, displacing the effects of the kingdom of darkness and bringing restoration. Our faithfulness to carry our assignments is how we release the justice of Heaven:

We are partnering with God to bring justice to the earth. It reverses every effect of sin and death in people's lives because it is the justice of restoration. Like Paul, we are restoring the knowledge of the one true God. Like Gideon, we are restoring the supernatural signs of God. We're restoring health to people's bodies, souls and spirits. We're restoring relationships and families. We're restoring financial prosperity. We're restoring morality in the government. We're restoring holiness in the arts. We're restoring the land and much more.

We still haven't seen all the effects of sin reversed in the world around us because the power of the Cross is only accessed through faith. Faith sees the finished work of the Cross in eternity and contends to see it released in history. We have to contend for it because there is resistance...We have an enemy who comes to steal, kill, and destroy (Vallotton, 144).

❧ Have you received a call from God to do something that seems totally irrational from the world's perspective? Or, do you dream of doing something that's never been done before? How are you pursuing this call or dream? What might be holding you back from stepping into it?

_____

_____

_____

❧ What is an area of injustice that you have been exposed to and are passionate to see changed? Have you received any strategies from the Lord for seeing Heaven's justice invade earth? Who will be affected by the breakthrough of justice in this area?

_____

_____

_____

❧ What is an area in your life where you have had to contend for breakthrough? What did you learn about your authority and identity as a believer through this process? How has this area of breakthrough shaped the way that you minister to others?

_____

_____

_____

SPIRITUAL WARFARE

One of the reasons many Christians have felt powerless in the face of injustice is that they lack training in their identity and ability to wage spiritual warfare...As Ephesians 6:12 (NKJV) reminds us, "For we do not wrestle against flesh and blood, but against principalities, against powers, against the rulers of the darkness of this age, against the spiritual hosts of wickedness in the heavenly places." This means that while our national government addresses injustice by means of court trials and waging physical wars, the Church addresses the roots of injustice in the spiritual realm. When we look at the darkness of our cities and nations, we understand that locking criminals behind bars won't satisfy justice. Justice will only come when the Kingdom of God displaces the spiritual hosts of wickedness in the heavenly realms (Vallotton, 145-146).

One of the most intriguing stories about spiritual warfare is found in Acts 19:

*Now **God worked** unusual miracles by the hands of Paul, so that even handkerchiefs or aprons were brought from his body to the sick, and the diseases left them and the evil spirits went out of them. Then some of the itinerant Jewish **exorcists took it upon themselves** to call the Name of the Lord Jesus over those who had evil spirits, saying, "We exorcise you by the Jesus whom Paul preaches." Also there were seven sons of Sceva, a Jewish chief priest, who did so. And the evil spirit answered and said, "Jesus I know, and Paul I know; but who are you?" Then the man in whom the evil spirit was leaped on them, overpowered them, and prevailed against them, so that they fled out of that house naked and wounded (Acts 19:11-16).*

This provides a clear picture of the difference between the spiritual warfare that *God* wages through our cooperation and the warfare that many people "take upon themselves." A huge difference between Paul and the sons of Sceva was that Paul had a relationship with the Christ in whose name he was healing people and casting out demons, while they did not. Our relationships with God, particularly our love and worship, are God's primary strategy for defeating the enemy. He could have wiped out the devil and his angels easily after they fell from Heaven, but He elected to raise up a family of sons and daughters who would fulfill the task that satan failed at, and who would worship Him and subdue the earthly kingdom through intimacy with Him. The most powerful kind of spiritual warfare we can engage in is choosing to love and serve God, not going out and chasing the devil. After all, he doesn't deserve that kind of attention.

Love is more powerful than hatred. Light is more powerful than the dark. Peace is more powerful than anger. Joy is more powerful than despair. These are the weapons with which we confront the works of the enemy. When we see problems in the world around us, we are not to fixate on them, but to move in the opposite spirit and access the more-than-adequate solutions to these problems in the Kingdom of God:

> As Christians, we wage most of our "warfare" by doing things that don't look like fighting. We prophesy blessing and destiny over people and cities. We love people sacrificially and bless them when they curse us. We pray for Heaven to come to earth (Vallotton, 154).

🙞 One of the biggest ways we have to wrestle with the powers of darkness is by refusing to let them distract us from our focus on loving God. What sorts of things have you experienced that work to distract you from keeping your eyes on the Lord? What strategies have you learned to recognize these distractions and resist them?

_____

_____

_____

_____

🙞 What is one area of your life or community in which the Lord has invited you to contend for justice? Do you recognize the spiritual influences at work, and if so, what is the opposite Kingdom influence? How does God want you to be a part of releasing this influence?

_____

_____

_____

_____

CONCLUSION

Scripture records that Jesus was "moved with compassion" for those around Him when He saw the injustices in their lives (see Matt. 9:36). Invite the Holy Spirit to infuse your spirit today with His compassion and passion to see the justice He has already paid for become a reality for those around you.

Chapter 13

THE DOGS OF DOOM STAND AT THE DOORS OF DESTINY

LIVING FROM ETERNITY

The survival mentality is a finite core value that restricts the impact of our lives to the here-and-now and robs us of the historic exploits that have been assigned to each of us by God Himself...Just imagine what a whole army of living "dead" people can accomplish when they are no longer intimidated by the grave, but are filled with the boldness of God! Royal people live from eternity and therefore don't view physical death as an end, but as an entrance to a new dimension in God...I am convinced that true courage is only born in those who have dealt with the fear of death...People who have dealt with death are dangerous. You can't stop them because there is nothing else to threaten them with (Vallotton, 156-158).

 REEDOM from the fear of death requires a different perspective on death. This different perspective is expressed by the apostle Paul when he speaks of our dying as something that has *already happened*:

*If then you **were raised** with Christ, seek those things which are above, where Christ is, sitting at the right hand of God. Set your mind on things above, not on things on the earth. For **you died,** and your life is hidden with Christ in God. When Christ who is our life appears, then you also will appear with Him in glory (Colossians 3:1-4).*

As you can see, it is our responsibility to focus on this superior truth of our life in Christ and allow it to shape our perspective and attitudes toward our daily circumstances. In his letter to the Philippians, Paul explained how this perspective on life and death shaped his attitude in the midst of the persecution he suffered in fulfilling his earthly calling:

> *For I know that this will turn out for my deliverance through your prayer and the supply of the Spirit of Jesus Christ, according to my earnest expectation and hope and that in nothing I shall be ashamed, but with **all boldness,** as always, so now also Christ will be magnified in my body, whether by life or by death. For to me, to live is Christ, and to die is gain* (Philippians 1:19-21).

Notice that Paul's freedom from the fear of death did not lead him to the attitude that his job on earth was simply to survive until he died or Jesus returned. That's not what "setting our minds on things above" means (see Col. 3:2). Instead, it made him bold in fulfilling the commission he had received from the Lord and joyful in the midst of his sufferings. Likewise, godly courage comes to those who have embraced an eternal perspective as well as answered the commission of God for them in this life.

Perhaps one of the most powerful pictures in Scripture of this holy boldness is in the response of Peter and John to persecution by the Jewish religious leaders after they healed the man at the Beautiful Gate:

> *Now when* [the Jewish leaders] *saw the **boldness** of Peter and John, and perceived that they were uneducated and untrained men, they marveled. And they realized that they had been with Jesus...So they called them and commanded them not to speak at all nor teach in the name of Jesus. But Peter and John answered and said to them, "Whether it is right in the sight of God to listen to you more than to God, you judge. For we cannot but speak the things which we have seen and heard"...So...* [the believers] *raised their voice to God with one accord and said..."Now, Lord, look on their threats, and grant to Your servants that with **all boldness** they may speak Your word, by stretching out Your hand to heal, and that signs and wonders may be done through the Name of Your holy Servant Jesus." And when they had prayed, the place where they were assembled together was shaken; and they were all filled with the Holy Spirit, and they spoke the word of God with **boldness** (Acts 4:13, 18-20, 24, 29-31).*

The fact that the disciples asked for *more boldness* after boldness was the thing that got them in trouble reveals that they truly were bold people. Where did this boldness come from? It came from hanging around Jesus. If you want the boldness that comes from overcoming the fear of death, or any fear for that matter, and connecting to the divine purpose of God for your life, then you should spend time with the Person who single-handedly defeated death and defined that purpose for you. This is what it means to "set our minds on things above, where Christ is." When you spend time in the presence of Christ, your heart will begin to burn for the things He cares about. You will also begin to see and hear things that you simply must talk about, no matter what people think. You will begin to see what an honor it is to be given the opportunity to emulate our Elder Brother and will courageously step into opportunities to see Him magnified.

&- The key statement in the disciples' response to the Jews was this: "Whether it is right in the sight of God to listen to you more than to God, you judge" (Acts 4:19). True freedom from fear and demonstrations of courage in your life all flow from the fact that you have decided to trust God's voice, will, presence, and power more than anything else. Why and how do you think faith is connected to courage?

&- Obviously, Heaven's response to the disciples' prayer of faith was a resounding, "Yes!" God is always ready to clothe us with Himself when we step toward His agenda—preaching and demonstrating the gospel of the Kingdom. Would you say that in your life you are taking risks that require this kind of supernatural courage? If so, have you been praying like the disciples and seeing results? If not, why?

THE DOORS OF DESTINY

If we take up a defensive posture, we actually yield the position of influence and authority that God has called us to have over the enemy. In the vacuum we've left, others who have found a cause worth dying for will rise up with conviction and power from the dark side. Then the great adventure is replaced with a boring and monotonous existence. Fear debilitates us from fighting the good fight that God has called us to. It has been disguised in the Church as "stewardship," "wisdom," and a bunch of other spiritual words, reducing the Christian experience to simply holding the fort. The only convictions that are worth living for are those worth dying for (Vallotton, 160).

The reality is that unless we have been possessed by our calling in God, we will naturally take up a defensive posture. Our God-given assignment—first to walk in relationship with Him as a son or daughter and then to become a mature expression of Christ in whatever realm to which God has called us—is what fuels our purpose and empowers us to take a proactive posture in life. However, the reality is that the enemy understands the destiny of the sons and daughters even better than many of them do, and so works to intimidate them most in the very areas where they are destined to be great:

"The dogs of doom stand at the doors of our destiny!" What we believe to be our most fearful stumbling block is actually the door to our greatest victory. Our greatest destiny lies on the other side of fear. Courage is the ability to advance in the face of adversity to obtain these treasures (Vallotton, 163).

❧ What is your "most fearful stumbling block?" Has it ever occurred to you that this issue came into your life to keep you from becoming who you were meant to be? What aspects of your calling in God does it work to keep you from?

_____

_____

_____

_____

David declared, "I sought the Lord, and He heard me, and delivered me from all my fears" (Psalm 34:4). A few verses later he said, "Oh, fear the Lord, you His saints! There is no want to those who fear Him" (Psalm 34:9). Apparently there is a fear that God wants to deliver us from, and a righteous fear of Him that we need. Anything that we fear more than God is actually an idol, for we've made it more powerful than God in our minds, which means that we have believed a lie. What are some of the lies you have believed that are designed to keep you from your destiny? Have you repented for believing these things and embraced the truth, and if so, what has the fruit been in your life?

_____

_____

_____

_____

OVERCOMING

The apostle John wrote, "They overcame him because of the blood of the Lamb and because of the word of their testimony, and they did not love their life even when faced with death" (Rev. 12:11)...**They overcame him by the blood of the Lamb:** This means we live from His victory instead of trying to get victory. Christians are to be offensively minded. We have the ball. The war has already been won and the only thing that remains is to fight the battles that enforce the victory. The devil has already been defeated. Jesus knocked his teeth out of his mouth. What is he going to do to you, gum you to death? (Vallotton, 164)

Look at Jesus' last words to His disciples:

In the world you will have tribulation; but be of good cheer, I have overcome the world (John 16:33).

The word *tribulation* here literally means "to press." There is resistance and conflict in our lives that create pressure. The question is: what are we made of? Bill Johnson often points out, "The same sun that melts the ice hardens the clay." Pressure can crush rock or create diamonds. It all depends on the material.

Jesus told us to be happy people whose joy comes from confidence that Jesus has already won. This is what it looks like to be "wise as serpents and harmless as doves" (Matthew 10:16). We grow wise as we encounter the pressures of the world around us—whether they are our own personal traumas designed to dislodge us from our destiny and faith or the brokenness of the world around us—and constantly bring these realities *under* the blood of Jesus and the victory of the Cross. In particular, we have to believe that the Cross is bigger than our own personal weakness, which naturally gets exposed by the pressures around us. The most responsible thing we can do when we encounter a problem, whether in us our outside of us, is not to ignore it or fixate on it, but to go to God and find out what He wants to do about it.

Jesus prayed, "I do not pray that You [Father] should take them out of the world, but that You should keep them from the evil one" (John 17:15). God's heart is for us to discover what we are made of, to realize that He has kept us in this world, not to crush us, but because the pressure of the world around us is actually a *necessary ingredient* for us to mature into our destiny. It doesn't mean that when something bad happens, God is behind it, but that God is in you and for you and has a solution. And the more you partner with Him to bring the solutions, the more authority and power He will entrust you with to extend the borders of His Kingdom in the world around you.

Where are you experiencing pressure in your life right now? Are you able to respond to these things with joy, or do you feel anxious and stressed? How can you bring these things under the victory of the Cross?

Every minute of your life has divine purpose. God put you on this planet and He wants you right here, right now. How does this confidence give you courage to confront the problems in front of you?

PEACE

Bill Johnson says, "You only have power over the storm you can sleep in"...The Lord spoke to me and told me that I was going to "learn the power of peace." I remembered Paul's words to the Philippians: "You are in no way alarmed by your opponents—which is a sign of destruction for them, but of salvation for you, and that too, from God" (Philippians 1:28). There is just something about courage that causes the enemy to know that he is already defeated, because courage is immune to his primary weapon, which is fear. Courage is peace in the storm, the inability to be alarmed by the enemy. When we can sleep in the storm, be calm in the face of battle and not panic in the midst of opposition, we have broken the back of the devil! (Vallotton, 166-167)

Like Jesus, we have been called to be peacemakers who calm the storms around us. But we can only face the "giants in the land" when we have first confronted the giant of fear in our own hearts. Paul declared:

For God has not given us a spirit of fear, but of power and of love and of a sound mind (2 Timothy 1:7).

We conquer fear in our lives by allowing the Spirit of God within us, the spirit of power, love, and a sound mind, to reign over every thought and action. The Kingdom must come within us before it can flow through us, as Jesus said, "The Kingdom of God is within you" (Luke 17:21). And Paul declared, "The Kingdom of God is not eating and drinking, but righteousness and peace and joy *in the Holy Spirit*" (Rom. 14:17). This is why Bill Johnson often explains that peace is not the absence of conflict, but the presence of the Spirit of Christ, the Prince of Peace.

☙ If you are feeling overwhelmed or intimidated by something in your life, does it occur to you that the first issue you must deal with is what is going on inside of you before you can deal with the problem? Why is it more responsible to go to God and get delivered of fear and anxiety than to try and deal with things in a fearful state?

_____

_____

_____

_____

_____

CONCLUSION

Invite the Spirit of Peace to reign in your heart today. Remember, Scripture commands us to be anxious for nothing, but to give everything to God so that His peace can come and guard our hearts and minds (Phil. 4:6-7). Then ask Him to fill you with boldness, just as He did in Acts 4, so that you can face the pressures around you, keep your eyes fixed on your divine purpose, and step courageously into the opportunities ahead of you today to see Christ magnified in your life.

Chapter 14

HIS MAJESTY'S SECRET SERVICE

OUR COMMISSION

There is an obvious difference between discipling people and discipling nations (Vallotton, 174).

ET'S consider some of these differences. Nations are made up of people, so discipling people is obviously part of discipling nations. But understanding that we've been commissioned to disciple nations should have a significant effect on *how* we disciple people.

Jesus chose twelve disciples. He trained them to do everything He did and sent them out to change the world. His choice reflects that Jesus knows exactly *how* nations could be changed. By and large, social change does not begin on the national level, but on the grassroots level. As Margaret Mead said, "Never doubt that a small group of committed people can change the world. It is the only thing that ever has."

The difference between a church that is discipling people and a church that is discipling nations really comes down to vision. There is something about the bigger vision of discipling nations that draws out our royal potential, not only by redirecting our focus from getting to Heaven to getting Heaven here, but also by training us to see the true impact and importance of touching the person in front of us. When one person gets saved, healed, and delivered, it's not just a great story. It's the Kingdom of our God advancing on the earth. As Isaiah prophesied, "Of the increase of His government and peace there will be no end" (Isa. 9:7).

This is why every believer is responsible to understand the big picture of God's purposes on the earth—to understand the true story of History:

> The fact that the Church has been restored to man's original position of dominion on earth requires us to learn and carry out the responsibilities that come with our authority. What is the purpose of our dominion? We are called

to fulfill the original commission given to Adam and Eve, but the task is different because we must not just subdue the earth but restore it from centuries of destruction it has suffered under the devil's tyranny. The Church is called to destroy every work of the devil, as Jesus modeled, to make disciples of the nations and to teach the world to obey the commands of Christ (Vallotton, 180).

When you received Christ and embraced the journey of discipleship, were you taught that your destiny was to change the world? What were you taught about the main goals of being a Christian? How has this influenced your perspective on your destiny?

_____

_____

_____

_____

One of the primary differences between a leader and a follower is that a leader is always aware of how his or her actions are on display and how he or she is influencing the surrounding environment. What are some of the ways that the responsibility to influence people and disciple nations should change our perspective and alter our priorities?

_____

_____

_____

_____

❧ If we are to train people to do everything Christ commanded, then we are to train them to be people who are also equipped to train others. What are some of the differences in the priorities of someone who is training a person to lead and someone who is training a person to follow? How did Jesus train His disciples to lead and in turn train others to lead?

_____

_____

_____

TRAINING NATIONS

When we received Jesus as Lord and Savior, we were given the kingdom!...In the last days the Church will be the chief authority on how to live life and make decisions. This will result in the nations coming to us and learning God's ways (Vallotton, 178-179).

Many leaders today have been emphasizing the difference between the *gospel of salvation* and the gospel Jesus commanded us to preach: the *gospel of the Kingdom*. The gospel of salvation focuses on getting people saved so they can go to Heaven, leading people to believe that once you're saved, you've reached your goal for this life and are just responsible to be a good person until you die. In the gospel of the Kingdom, salvation is the doorway into an entirely new life. The *good news* in this gospel is that God has made it possible for you to become His son or daughter and to partner with your Father in seeing His dominion expressed in every area of life and society.

The realm of the Kingdom contains the blueprint for all of creation as well as every resource required for people to live life as God intended. This means that our responsibility as believers is not simply to conquer the works of darkness in our land, but also to establish the *order* of God there. This is why, once again, Jesus emphasized over and over that one of our highest privileges and responsibilities as sons and daughters of God is to *ask*, *seek*, and *knock*. We are the ones who have access to the creative ideas and answers of the Kingdom, and we are to be zealous in pursuing them. God wants His kids to start dreaming about what the world could look like when His Kingdom is fully expressed in every area of life.

There are several implications of the gospel of the Kingdom that should be founded in our thinking. First, we must not compartmentalize our lives into "spiritual" things and "non-spiritual" things. There is no sacred and secular in the Kingdom—it's all sacred. Second, it is our responsibility to take the mundane activities of our life and offer them to God. It is also our responsibility to seek our Father's Kingdom—to learn His ways, grow to understand what His Kingdom is like, and bring our life and all our pursuits into alignment with that Kingdom. Consider:

Therefore, whether you eat or drink, or whatever you do, do all to the glory of God (1 Corinthians 10:31).

Therefore do not worry, saying "What shall we eat?" or "What shall we drink?" or "What shall we wear?" For after all these things the Gentiles seek. For your heavenly Father knows that you need all these things. But seek first the kingdom of God and His righteousness, and all these things shall be added to you (Matthew 6:31-33).

Giving things to God sanctifies them for His purposes. Have you ever felt that there was something you were passionate about but felt wasn't particularly spiritual? Have you given it to God? What might that area of interest look like if the reality of the Kingdom of God began to be expressed?

The fact that every disciple of Christ is called to disciple others means that we are not only to be learners but also to be teachers. Jesus set the example for us by demonstrating that teachers teach with both words and demonstrations that support the truth of those words. Why is it important for us to experience and demonstrate the reality of the Kingdom if we are destined to teach the nations about the Kingdom?

A ROYAL PRIESTHOOD

If we are going to wake up and take ownership of our communities, we will by necessity confront the individualism around us and in us. One way to get a glimpse of our true attitude regarding our responsibility is to ask ourselves if we treat every person we meet like family. Jesus taught us to pray with a corporate prayer addressed to "Our Father," which reveals God's desire for His people to identify with the situations of their neighbors and community as if they were all in the family of God. We must let a sense of ownership permeate the way we think about the land and community around us. When we begin to identify ourselves with the future of our cities, we will start praying prayers that will shift the spiritual atmosphere and bring the kingdom of Heaven (Vallotton, 182).

Have you noticed that in a culture that prizes individualism, more often than not this individualism doesn't lead people to believe they can change the world, but they pretend the world isn't there? If life is all about you, then your vision is just too small, and you won't be inspired to do anything great. As much as many of us want to find our own destinies, there's something in us that knows that it is our destiny to be caught up in something bigger than ourselves.

There is nothing bigger and yet more personally fulfilling than being a son or daughter of God. And as such, we have a dual role. We are not only kings, but also *priests*:

> *To Him who loved us and washed us from our sins in His own blood, and has made us* **kings and priests** *to His God and Father, to Him be glory and dominion forever and ever* (Revelation 1:5-6).

> *You were slain, and have redeemed us to God by Your blood out of every tribe and tongue and people and nation, and have made us* **kings and priests** *to our God; and* **we shall reign on the earth** (Revelation 5:9b-10).

What is a priest? Throughout the Scriptures, priests did two primary things. They ministered to God on behalf of man, and ministered to man on behalf of God. (Often both these tasks were fulfilled in the same action. For example, the priests made animal sacrifices for sin. Through the act of sacrifice, atonement was made for sin, a ministry to God, and forgiveness for sin was given, a ministry to man. See Leviticus 4.) Notice that both tasks are representational, or *intercessory*. This means that the priest was never really doing anything just by himself or for himself. His whole life was lived in the service of others.

In the Old Testament, the priests interceded between God and man through the Temple ministry of sacrifices and rituals. In the New Testament, Jesus became our High Priest by offering Himself as a sacrifice for our sin and restoring sons to His Father. And as the priesthood of God, believers are called to intercede for man on behalf of the Lord. As Paul declared:

> *Now all things are of God, who has reconciled us to Himself through Jesus Christ, and has given us the ministry of reconciliation, that is, that God was in Christ reconciling the world to Himself, not imputing their trespasses to them, and has*

committed to us the word of reconciliation. Now then, we are ambassadors for Christ, as though God were pleading through us: we implore you on Christ's behalf, be reconciled to God (2 Corinthians 5:18-20).

Now that our sin has been paid for, our ministry to God doesn't require us to be dealing with the sin issue all the time; we primarily minister to Him in worship. But there is something about the fact that we're following a Man who paid the price for a debt He didn't incur. And He told us, "Greater love has no one than this, than to lay down one's life for his friends" (John 15:13). Notice that Christ laid His life down for the whole world. He didn't shut anyone out from being His friend, but made us all the objects of His love. Christ's example should move us to love *all people* and to intercede for those who have not yet experienced the grace that is available for them. We don't have to beg God to show mercy; He already has. Our job is to try to help position people to receive that mercy. There are ways that we can intercede for people before God as priests. For one, we have this statement of Christ:

If you forgive the sins of any, they are forgiven them (John 20:23).

If this verse has an implication for us as priests, it would seem to be that our forgiveness of people is a key to putting the forgiveness that God has already given them in Christ into their account. Because all sin is truly against God, this authority to forgive sins does not rest upon us only when someone has sinned against us. What could be the impact of a Church that actively forgives individuals, cities, and nations of sin?

_____

_____

_____

_____

_____

❧ Do you recognize that you primarily think of people in the Church as "us" and people outside the Church as "them"? What are some possible consequences of this mentality that would hinder you from operating in your priestly role?

_____

_____

_____

_____

_____

_____

_____

CONCLUSION

We know where history is heading. One day we shall see the fullness of the declaration that, "The kingdoms of this world have become the kingdoms of our Lord and of His Christ, and He shall reign forever and ever!" (Rev. 11:15). But that "becoming" process is going to happen through Christ's plan—"This *gospel of the Kingdom* will be preached in all the world as a witness to all the nations, and then the end will come" (Matt. 24:14). We are the generation commissioned to preach this gospel of the Kingdom and bring the kingdoms of the world into the Kingdom of God—to implore people to be reconciled to God and to demonstrate the superior reality of His world.

Spend some time with the Holy Spirit today asking Him about your part in discipling the nations.

Chapter 15

PASSING THE BATON

INHERITANCE

Inheritance makes each generation responsible to both receive and honor what has passed on from the previous generation, and then pay their own price to make it grow so that the next generation starts ahead of them. The ceiling of one generation must become the floor of the next. In our lifetime, this requires us to act with an awareness that our actions affect generations ahead of us. This is precisely the effect that righteousness will have on the way we think, because "a righteous man leaves an inheritance to his children's children" (Vallotton, 188).

❧ Why do you think righteousness causes us to think and care, not only about the people around us, but about the people we will never meet but who will be affected by our lives?

_____

_____

_____

"Revelation," or the "things which are revealed," is the inheritance of the Kingdom...If revelation is meant to be the inheritance of the Kingdom, it is clear that God intends for more than information to be passed on to the next generation. The fruit of revelation is personal transformation and supernatural demonstrations of the nature of God. Therefore, the inheritance of revelation is the inheritance of models, heroes who became a revelation of God's nature, and the testimonies of their teaching and exploits (Vallotton, 189-190).

Can you imagine what Hebrews 11 would sound like if the people in the "Hall of Faith" had only *told* their children about the goodness and power of God? Do you think that their testimonies still would have been passed down for thousands of years? Probably not. The stories that have power are the stories of people who believed God in their actions as well as their hearts and minds.

All Christian parents want to leave legacies of faith in God, to see their children come to know and follow Him. But the most powerful inheritance we can give to them and those around us is to *show* them what God is like.

☙ Who is a role model in your life—a Bible character, historical figure, ancestor, family member, teacher, leader, and so forth—who modeled the nature of Christ in some dimension that you wish to emulate? What aspects of Christ's nature are you passionate about showing to those around you? What happens when people try to pass on revelation about God that they are not endeavoring to demonstrate?

_____

_____

_____

_____

INHERITANCE COMES FROM FATHERS AND MOTHERS

The root of the word "testimony" is a word that means "do again." Every time we repeat the stories of God's invasions into human history, we are calling Him to reveal Himself as the same God today. For this reason, we cannot truly receive our spiritual inheritance if we mean only to applaud the accomplishments of our ancestors. We do not honor the memory of God's heroes by just remembering them. We only honor them if we imitate them by coming to know the God they knew and calling Him to bring His kingdom in our day (Vallotton, 191).

Paul looms large in the New Testament, especially since he wrote most of it. Not only was he a brilliant thinker, speaker, and writer, he was a fearless adventurer, hard-working business-man, and a miracle worker. His salvation testimony is one of the most dramatic and powerful in the whole Bible, and has since given faith to every believer that God can save the most violent God-haters in the land. He is a great hero of the faith. But it is only through purposing to imitate him and invite God to repeat the testimony of Paul's life in ours that we can truly receive Paul's inheritance and become true sons and daughters of this spiritual father.

One of the biggest things that Paul has left the body of believers as an inheritance is the testimony of what true spiritual fatherhood (and motherhood) looks like. His letters expressed the heart of a father for his spiritual children, and instructed them on what it looks like to receive the spiritual inheritance he was giving to them. Since we are called both to receive and leave an inheritance, to be discipled and to disciple, this instruction is invaluable and extremely practical for us.

Let's consider three of the things that Paul taught us about inheritance. First of all, Paul understood the nature of the testimony and the importance of his sons and daughters coming to have their own encounters with God. In the case of the Corinthian church, he intentionally created an opportunity for them to encounter God in this way:

> *And I, brethren, when I came to you, did not come with excellence of speech or of wisdom declaring to you the testimony of God. For I determined not to know any-thing among you except Jesus Christ and Him crucified. I was with you in weakness, in fear, and in much trembling. And my speech and my preaching were not with persuasive words of human wisdom, but in demonstration of the Spirit and of power, that your faith should not be in the wisdom of men but in the power of God* (1 Corinthians 2:1-5).

A true father or mother in the faith, like Paul, is someone who doesn't draw the focus to self, but instead *facilitates* God encounters. On several occasions, Paul actually prays in his letters for us to encounter God. What would happen if we took hold of this inheritance and engaged our faith in receiving what this father asked of God?

Second, Paul corrected his spiritual children. After correcting the Corinthians, he said:

> *I do not write these things to shame you, but as my beloved children I warn you. For though you might have ten thousand instructors in Christ, yet you do*

not have many fathers; for in Christ Jesus I have begotten you through the gospel (1 Corinthians 4:14-15).

The writer of Hebrews, who quite possibly was Paul, expressed this aspect of true godly parenting:

You have forgotten the exhortation which speaks to you as to sons: "My son, do not despise the chastening of the Lord, nor be discouraged when you are rebuked by Him; for whom the Lord loves He chastens, and scourges every son whom He receives." If you endure chastening, God deals with you as with sons; for what son is there whom a father does not chasten? But if you are without chastening, of which all have become partakers, then you are illegitimate and not sons. Furthermore, we have had human fathers who corrected us, and we paid them respect. Shall we not much more readily be in subjection to the Father of spirits and live? (Hebrews 12:5-9)

Finally, Paul exhorted his sons and daughters to get out there and fulfill their destinies. He instructed Timothy:

*This charge I commit to you, son Timothy, according to the prophecies previously made concerning you, that by them you may wage the good warfare, having faith and a good conscience...Let no one despise your youth, but be an example to the believers in word, in conduct, in love, in spirit, in faith, in purity. Till I come, give attention to reading, to exhortation, to doctrine. **Do not neglect the gift that is in you,** which was given to you by prophecy with the laying on of the hands of the elder-ship. Meditate on these things; give yourself entirely to them, that your progress may be evident to all...Therefore I remind you to **stir up the gift of God which is in you** through the laying on of my hands* (1 Timothy 1:18-19; 4:12-15; 2 Timothy 1:6).

Paul clearly believed that we can receive spiritual gifts and graces through impartation from our spiritual fathers. But his point to Timothy was that these impartations have to be used!

In conclusion, we receive a spiritual inheritance when we step toward the encounters with God that have been prepared for us through the testimony of the lives of our spiritual fathers, when we allow ourselves to be disciplined and corrected by their wisdom and insight, and when we use the gifts that have been imparted to us.

❧ Why is correction a valuable inheritance to receive from parents? Have you benefited from the correction of true spiritual parents who have disciplined you in love and given you wisdom for walking in your destiny?

_____

_____

_____

❧ When you read of the great faith exploits of believers from the past, how does it affect you? Would your perspective change if you thought of these people as fathers and mothers who are rooting for you to believe God too? What is a testimony that you are passionate to see God "do again" in your lifetime?

_____

_____

_____

HIDDEN FOR US

God hides things for us because, "It is the glory of God to conceal a matter, but the glory of kings is to search out a matter" (Proverbs 25:2). God is glorified by not speaking in plain language to you. He's actually glorified by speaking in parables and symbols and dark sayings. And because the glory of kings is to search out a matter, the royalty that exists in the life of the believer comes to the surface when we realize we have legal access to hidden things and we begin to pursue the unlocking of those mysteries. Those who sit back and say, "Well, whatever God wants me to have I'm happy to receive," are living a pauper's lifestyle in a kingly mansion (Vallotton, 197).

Could it be that life in the Kingdom is designed as a grand game of Hide and Seek? Or is it like a cosmic Christmas morning, with endless miles of gifts waiting under the tree for all of us? It may sound silly to talk about our destiny in these terms, but at the same time, imagining it like that helps us to get in touch with certain feelings—excitement, anticipation, and intense curiosity. Some of us also know the joy of buying the perfect gift for someone and then unveiling it at the perfect moment—when it's just what he or she always wanted. Maybe that is the joy our Father has in hiding things for us. Maybe the royalty He is trying to draw to the surface in us is that intense joy, curiosity, and anticipation for what He has in store for us. It certainly makes sense that the King's glory and our glory are most clearly seen in the dance of our intimacy, love, and relationship.

&- Why is it so important to understand that God does not hide things from us but for us? What are some of the unexpected ways that God has spoken to you? Have you received a word from God that you didn't understand and pursued the mystery until it was unlocked for you? How did this affect your relationship with God?

_____

_____

_____

_____

_____

&- What aspects of God and the Kingdom ignite your curiosity?

_____

_____

_____

_____

INHERITANCE THROUGH HONOR

"He who receives a prophet in the name of a prophet shall receive a prophet's reward"(Matthew 10:41)...The Lord takes it personally when we honor the Christ in someone else...There are mantles, realms of God, revelations, and levels of anointing that (people operate) in that we have access to, simply by honoring. We must embrace our opportunity and responsibility to honor those men and women in history who have broken into different realms of God and advanced the Kingdom, as well as to honor those around us. Honoring those around us doesn't just mean the people with big names. The real challenge is to learn how to know one another after the Spirit so we can recognize the gifts and anointing that God has given to each of the members of His Body. The Lord Jesus, through the apostle Paul, said we're to submit to one another in the fear of Christ. That means we are to honor the Christ in each other (Vallotton, 198-199).

There is something we learn about honor here, and that is that it is important to acknowledge the gifts of God on a person verbally. We are to receive a prophet "in the name of a prophet" if we want to receive a prophet's reward. Calling out the gifts and anointing that we see in one another is a key ingredient in receiving grace from one another. Obviously, we must be able to discern those things in order to call them out, but we will have a much better chance if we are looking for them and expecting that God has hidden an inheritance in the life of every one of His kids.

🙠 Has anyone ever honored you by verbally acknowledging the gifts of God in your life? If so, how did this experience affect you? How did it affect the expression of these gifts?

_____

_____

_____

_____

_____

❧ What does it mean to know one another after the Spirit? Do you look for the gifts and anointing in the lives of your brothers and sisters? Do you acknowledge what you see, and if so, how has this affected you and those around you?

_____

_____

_____

_____

_____

_____

CONCLUSION

Do we know why we're surrounded by a cloud of witnesses?...They're all waiting to see what we will do with what we've been given (Vallotton, 201).

Here is the conclusion that the writer of Hebrews comes to in this situation:

Therefore we also, since we are surrounded by so great a cloud of witnesses, let us lay aside every weight, and the sin which so easily ensnares us, and let us run with endurance the race that is set before us (Hebrews 12:1).

Spend time asking the Holy Spirit about the kind of legacy you want to leave to your children, grandchildren, and great-grandchildren in the faith. Consider starting a journal in which to record the testimonies you have seen and the wisdom you wish to impart.

Chapter 16

BUILDING STRATEGIC ALLIANCES WITH HEAVENLY ALLIES

APOSTLES AND APOSTOLIC MISSION

We need to make sure we're submitted to those the Lord has placed in authority over us, because when the Bride of Christ is under authority, the angels recognize our authority and accomplish the words of our prayers and prophecies (see Psalm 103:20). When we submit to the mission of Heaven, we commission the angels to carry out the word of the Lord.

Do the angels always go out and answer everyone's prayers and prophecies? I don't believe they do, because I believe they recognize people who are under submission to an apostolic mission. This is just a theory, but I think sometimes people pray the right prayers when they're in trouble, but their life isn't in submission and so the situation doesn't change. They want to have the benefits of the kingdom, but they don't want to serve the King. I don't mean they're going to hell, but they haven't recognized and submitted to the people that the Lord has delegated to have spiritual authority in their lives (Vallotton, 206).

NOTICE that submission to the King, submission to the mission of Heaven, submission to an apostolic mission, and submission to the Lord's delegated authority are all related here. Let's consider just what it is that we are to submit to before we address the issue of submission itself. Most believers should know what it means to submit to God, since conversion began with an act of submission. But it's the issue of submission to other people that many stumble over. Let's consider:

God has designed and commissioned a government for His Royal Priesthood. Its purpose is to equip the saints for the work of the ministry so we grow into the "measure of the stature of the fullness of Christ" (Eph. 4:13).

Paul describes this government or structure thus:

> *Now, therefore, you are no longer strangers and foreigners, but fellow citizens with the saints and members of the household of God, having been built on the **foundation of the apostles and prophets,** Jesus Christ Himself being the chief Cornerstone, in whom the whole building, being fitted together, grows into a holy temple in the Lord, in whom you also are being built together for a dwelling place of God in the Spirit* (Ephesians 2:19-22).

> *And God appointed these in the Church: first apostles, second prophets, third teachers, after that miracles, then gifts of healings, helps, administrations, varieties of tongues* (1 Corinthians 12:28).

> *And He Himself gave some to be apostles, some prophets, some evangelists, and some pastors and teachers, for the equipping of the saints for the work of ministry* (Ephesians 4:11-12).

When Jesus chose His twelve disciples and commissioned them to lead His Church, He called them all *apostles*. The term *apostle* simply means "a delegate, messenger, one sent forth with orders."[1] In short, it means someone who *has authority* because he or she is *under authority*. Jesus described how this flow of authority worked when He said:

> *Most assuredly, I say to you, he who receives whomever I send receives Me; and he who receives Me receives Him who sent Me* (John 13:20).

This dynamic is true of all believers. Christ sends all of us into the world as His ambassadors. But each of us must go through a process of learning to walk under authority and carry authority, and this process requires the equipping of those Christ has specially appointed to distribute His grace to the Body.

An apostle is not a title; it is a role, and can be recognized by the functions of that role. The examples of apostles in Scripture, particularly the apostle Paul, indicate that one of the functions of the role of an apostle is to help to establish communities of believers who are seeking the Kingdom. In order to do this, an apostle must be equipped to articulate the big picture of a Kingdom worldview as well as demonstrate that reality through signs and wonders:

And they went out and preached everywhere, the Lord working with them and confirming the word through the accompanying signs (Mark 16:20).

Finally, because apostles have a Kingdom "blueprint", they have been specially equipped to recognize and designate other leaders and facilitate the process of equipping the saints. But notice that in Paul's description, apostles and prophets are the *foundation*. This means that they don't have a starring role, but a supporting role in the Church. A true apostle is not trying to promote his or her own agenda, but is passionately and boldly promoting the agenda of the Kingdom—on earth as it is in Heaven.

Submission to delegated authority and an apostolic mission comes down to two things; first, joining a group of believers who are led by an apostle (remember—it's a role, not a title, so don't necessarily look at what the leader is called); second, participating in the equipping process so that you can step into whatever aspect of the "work of the ministry" to which you've been called.

&- If this picture of how Christ has designed His body to function and grow under a certain order of leadership is unfamiliar to you, how is it different than what you've seen and experienced? If it is familiar to you, how has receiving the grace of an apostle equipped you for ministry?

_____

_____

_____

&- Who are the spiritual authorities that the Lord has specifically delegated in your life and how would you describe your relationship with them?

_____

_____

_____

SUBMISSION

Submission is a choice, an act of the will. It is not surrendering your will. Picture a salmon swimming upstream, struggling with all its might and making slow progress. Then it turns and begins to swim with the current. It is still swimming, but the momentum of the stream synergizes with its motions and it covers in no time the ground that took hours to cover in the opposite direction. This is what submission to an apostolic mission looks like. It's stepping into the flow of grace and cooperating with the administration Christ has established to distribute the benefits of the Kingdom to every member of His Body.

The writer of Hebrews declared:

> *Obey those who rule over you, and be submissive, for they watch out for your souls, as those who must give account. Let them do so with joy and not with grief, for that would be unprofitable for you* (Hebrews 13:17).

In other words, cooperation benefits everyone. Of course, in order to cooperate with our leaders, we must recognize them as leaders, understand their roles, and finally, trust them. We must remember that unless our leaders know more than we do and can do things we can't do, they can't lead us anywhere. But they also can't lead us unless we agree to follow. And those apostles...they're like Jesus! They want to go into uncharted territory. You need a spirit of adventure, fearlessness, and willingness to fail if you're going to follow an apostle. A pioneering spirit is the mark of an apostolic community of believers. The big vision of their leaders just leaks on everyone and they start burning to see untouched realms of life experience the reality of the Kingdom. After all, who wants to camp out and play church when you can change the world?

We must not allow the stories of fallen leaders to shake our faith, any more than we should allow the high incidence of divorce to shake our faith in God's design and purpose for marriage. The fact is that God still delegates men and women with power and authority to equip His saints. We must realize, as the verse above expresses, that our leaders need us just as we need them. This kind of submission and cooperation is expressed beautifully in the story of Joshua and Aaron holding up the arms of Moses. Moses had the favor, authority, and power of God, but lacked the physical strength to keep administering it. In submitting to and supporting their leader, Joshua and Aaron stepped into the flow of what God was doing and became an essential ingredient in bringing victory to Israel.

❧ What would you say is the most important quality of a Christian leader? Would you say that it's important for the Body of Christ to be led by pioneers, and if so, why?

_____

_____

_____

❧ How do you support your leader and your leader's vision? Do you belong to a community of believers that knows how to hold up the arms of its leaders, and if so, how has this cooperation affected the community?

_____

_____

_____

SUBMISSION AND PROMOTION

Joseph's personal victories became a corporate covering, but there is no victory without a battle. Battles are designed to free us from the prisons of life and take us to the palace of our destiny. Between the prison and the palace there is always a process that this warfare facilitates. The process is often better described as a trial. The trials of our life are designed to develop our character so that we can stay in the palace...this is the key to obtaining spiritual authority: submission until promotion (Vallotton, 207, 210).

The word for _trial_ in Greek means "the proving." Jesus Himself went through "the proving" directly after He was baptized and declared to be the Son of God by the Father Himself (see Luke 3:22; 4:1-13). The enemy basically said, "You're the Son of God? Prove it." Significantly, Jesus' identity was "proven" by the fact that He didn't try to prove Himself. It was proven by His refusal to submit to any voice but God's. It was only after He was tested that He began to demonstrate the true proofs of the word over His life.

Throughout the New Testament, the trials we experience are specifically referred to as trials of our *faith*. Peter declared:

> *Now for a little while, if need be, you have been grieved by various trials, that the genuineness of your faith, being much more precious than gold that perishes, though it is tested by fire, may be found to praise, honor, and glory at the revelation of Jesus Christ* (1 Peter 1:6b-7).

The thing that proves *who we are* is whether or not we choose to listen to and believe God in every situation. Faith is an act of submission because it's an act of trust. Part of the reason we can trust a tested leader and submit to his or her leadership is that every leader who has been proven faithful has *submitted* to God under pressure. *Only people who know how to submit to God's authority can carry it.*

❧ Describe an experience that tested your faith in what God has said to you. Did you recognize this trial of your faith for what it was? How did this trial shape you into who you are and give you what you needed to walk through your present season of life?

_____

_____

_____

_____

❧ What are some of the trials that your leaders have faced in order to succeed in the role they have now? In what ways do your leaders model submission to God?

_____

_____

_____

_____

Submitting to One Another

Paul instructs us many times in his letters to submit to one another as to Christ. There is an element of spiritual covering which is preserved as we honor our covenant with the Body of Christ and with one another as brothers and sisters in the Lord. The Lord calls us His Body because every member is dependent on the other and every choice we make affects the whole. If we choose to honor and serve the Body of Christ, we preserve the connection which brings life, blessing and protection to us (Vallotton, 213-214).

Believers practice mutual submission every time they give and receive love from one another. The royal family of God looks out for one another. We restore one another when we bear one another's burdens (see Gal. 6:1-2). We give and receive words of edification, exhortation, and comfort (1 Cor. 14:3). We protect our connections with each other, because Jesus instructed that doing so was part of protecting our connection with God:

Therefore if you bring your gift to the altar, and there remember that your brother has something against you, leave your gift there before the altar, and go your way. First be reconciled to your brother, and then come and offer your gift (Matthew 5:23-24).

John goes further:

In this the children of God and the children of the devil are manifest: Whoever does not practice righteousness is not of God, nor is he who does not love his brother. For this is the message that you heard from the beginning, that we should love one another...We know that we have passed from death to life, because we love the brethren. He who does not love his brother abides in death. Whoever hates his brother is a murderer, and you know that no murderer has eternal life abiding in him. By this we know love, because He laid down His life for us. And we also ought to lay down our lives for the brethren (1 John 3:10-11,14-16).

The sign that we possess eternal life, a relationship with the Spirit of God, and are sons of our Father is that we lay down our lives for our brothers. Expressing this in our thoughts, words, and actions is what fuels and protects our connection with both God and man.

How have breaches in your relationships with your brothers and sisters affected your relationship with God? Do you struggle with either receiving or giving love? How does this affect your relationship with God?

_____

_____

_____

_____

_____

_____

_____

Conclusion

Invite the Holy Spirit to take inventory of your relationships in the Body of Christ, both with leaders and fellow believers. Ask Him to give you keys for strengthening these relationships. Ask Him to expand the heart of Christ in you to lay down your life for your brothers.

Endnotes

1. Strong's Greek, accessed May 2008, taken from http://cf.blueletterbible.org/lang/lexicon/lexicon.cfm?Strongs=G652&t=KJV; s.v. "apostle."

2. Strong's Greek, accessed May 2008, taken from http://cf.blueletterbible.org/lang/lexicon/lexicon.cfm?Strongs=G1382&t=KJV; s.v. "trial."

Chapter 17

PRESERVING THE PLANET

THE CHURCH'S ROLE

The Church is the element in society that preserves the culture from the wrath of God and the destruction of evil forces. A great example of this is Joseph, who as we saw in the last chapter released a corporate blessing through his righteous life. His presence in Egypt caused the Israelites and the Egyptians to be spared from a worldwide famine...So what does it mean to become tasteless? It implies that we have stopped preserving the world. We have become tasteless when we prophesy against the people we are supposed to be preserving (Vallotton, 217-218).

 EFORE we consider the perversion in judging the world, let's look at some aspects of our preservative role on the earth. We often focus on the part in Paul's prayer for the Ephesians that talks about having our eyes enlightened to know the hope of our calling. But his prayer was also for us to receive the revelation of the Church's purpose in the world:

*I ask—ask the God of our Master, Jesus Christ, the God of glory—to make you intelligent and discerning in knowing Him personally, your eyes focused and clear, so that you can see exactly what it is He is calling you to do, grasp the immensity of this glorious way of life He has for His followers, oh, the utter extravagance of His work in us who trust Him—endless energy, boundless strength! All this energy issues from Christ: God raised Him from death and set Him on a throne in deep heaven, in charge of running the universe, everything from galaxies to governments, no name and no power exempt from His rule. And not just for the time being, but forever. He is in charge of it all, has the final word on everything. **At the center of all this, Christ rules the church. The church, you see, is not peripheral to the***

world; the world is peripheral to the church. The church is Christ's Body, in which He speaks and acts, by which He fills everything with His presence (Ephesians 1:17-23 The Message).

The Church is the presence of Christ on the earth. The fact that many of us in the Church are still trying to figure that out does not diminish that reality. This describes how the influence that the Church is to have in the world is not minimal or marginal but central. We have to begin to see ourselves as the outpost of the government of God, the government that is slowly and surely taking over the world, wherever we are. We have to see that Christ already possesses the territory around us. It is not the world's, nor the devil's! The Son of Man has purchased the entire realm of man's dominion, but He's asserting His rightful ownership only through the cooperation and agreement of those who are choosing His side freely. C.S. Lewis addressed the wisdom of this plan:

Why is God landing in this enemy-occupied world in disguise and starting a sort of secret society to undermine the devil? Why is He not landing in force, invading it? Is it that He is not strong enough? Well, Christians think He is going to land in force; we do not know when. But we can guess why He is delaying. He wants to give us the chance of joining His side freely. I do not suppose you and I would have thought much of a Frenchman who waited till the Allies were marching into Germany and then announced he was on our side. God will invade. But I wonder whether people who ask God to interfere openly and directly in our world quite realise what it will be like when He does. When that happens, it is the end of the world. When the author walks on to the stage the play is over. God is going to invade, all right: but what is the good of saying you are on His side then, when you see the whole natural universe melting away like a dream and something else—something it never entered your head to conceive—comes crashing in; something so beautiful to some of us and so terrible to others that none of us will have any choice left? For this time it will be God without disguise; something so overwhelming that it will strike either irresistible love or irresistible horror into every creature. It will be too late then to choose your side. There is no use saying you choose to lie down when it has become impossible to stand up. That will not be the time for choosing: it will be the time when we discover which side we really have chosen, whether we realised it before or not. Now, today, this moment, is our chance to choose the right side. God is holding back to give us that chance. It will not last forever. We must take it or leave it.[1]

It is *our job* to show the world what the "right side" is. How do we do this? By displaying *righteousness*. Righteousness flows from being in a right relationship with God; it describes a person whose heart and behavior are in alignment with God's and thus express His nature. The natural expression of a righteous person is to do "good works." "Good works" is the term that Jesus used to explain what He meant by *salt* and *light*:

> *Let your light so shine before men, that they may see your good works and glorify your Father in heaven* (Matthew 5:16).

Our good works actually cause the world to give glory to God. This is how we are going to lead the planet into its destiny and prepare people to encounter the Lord:

> *...having your conduct honorable among the Gentiles, that when they speak against you as evildoers, they may, by your good works which they observe, glorify God in the day of visitation* (1 Peter 2:12).

But we do not do good works in order to get a response from the world. The response that we care about is God's response:

> *We make it our aim, whether present or absent, to be well pleasing to Him. For we must all appear before the judgment seat of Christ, that each one may receive the things done in the body, according to what he has done, whether good or bad. Knowing, therefore, the terror of the Lord, we persuade men...For the love of Christ compels us, because we judge thus: that if One died for all, then all died; and He died for all, that those who live should live no longer for themselves, but for Him Who died for them and rose again. Therefore, from now on, we regard no one according to the flesh. Even though we have known Christ according to the flesh, yet now we know Him thus no longer* (2 Corinthians 5:9-11a; 14-16).

Paul doesn't make a distinction here between Christians and non-Christians. He says that "all died" with Christ (see 2 Cor. 5:14). It's hard to wrap our minds around, but the human race died and was resurrected in Him. It is true all have a choice to believe the truth and step into it, but Paul's point is that we have to see every person in front of us as someone, not only for whom Christ died, but who has already died with Christ. This is how we avoid regarding people according to the flesh. And notice the two things that motivated Paul—the love of God for people, and the weight of the fact that we are all going to give an account before God for our works. These two things, not the response of people, are what we are accountable for.

Notice that the "fear of the Lord" Paul talks about motivates him to love people and to persuade them, not by threatening them with hell, but by showing them Heaven. Why should the knowledge that we will give an account to God motivate us to love people?

JUDGE NOT

There are two things, among others, to consider when it comes to the issue of judgment. First of all, when we identify something as the judgment of God for sin, we are making a judgment. Jesus instructed:

> *Judge not, that you be not judged. For with what judgment you judge, you will be judged; and with the measure you use, it will be measured back to you* (Matthew 7:1-2).

We must shift our focus from getting to the bottom of why bad things happen to people, and spend our time and attention on what Christ has commanded us to do about it. We are not to condemn people, but forgive them. We are to show mercy and compassion. We are to let God be the judge and not try to usurp His role:

> *Beloved, do not avenge yourselves, but rather give place to wrath; for it is written, "Vengeance is Mine, I will repay," says the Lord. Therefore, "If your enemy is hungry, feed him; if he is thirsty, give him a drink; for in so doing you will heap coals of fire on his head." Do not be overcome by evil, but overcome evil with good* (Romans 12:19-21).

In other words our job is to love and forgive people, and when we do our part, God does His part to convict them. Otherwise, we are actually allowing ourselves to be overcome by evil. (As we've already seen, we also need to remember that our battle is not against flesh and blood, and the justice that God is bringing to the earth is not punishment but restoration.)

Now that Christ has satisfied the wrath of God for sin, God, for His part, is not at odds with humanity. God is working to be reconciled to humanity, as we read before:

> *Now all things are of God, who has reconciled us to Himself through Jesus Christ, and has given us the ministry of reconciliation, that is, that God was in Christ reconciling the world to Himself,* **not imputing their trespasses to them,** *and has committed to us the word of reconciliation* (2 Corinthians 5:18-19).

The fact that God is not imputing the sins of people to them means that He is not judging them for what they've done!

Bill Johnson often says that Jesus Christ is *perfect theology*. Colossians says that He is the "image of the invisible God" (Col. 1:15). In other words, if you don't see it in Jesus, it isn't in God. When people ask, "Well, what about Job? What about the angry God we see in the Old Testament?" Bill answers, "I'm not a disciple of Job. And what I know about the Old Testament was that it was written to reveal the problem. Jesus is the answer to the problem." Jesus said:

> *For God did not send His Son into the world to condemn the world, but that the world through Him might be saved* (John 3:17).

The ministry of Christ, pure and simple, is not the ministry of condemnation, but the ministry of salvation. It is this ministry that we have been called to walk in.

One thing that does help us understand the world around us is the fact that it is a world of consequences, of causes and effects. God calls it *sowing* and *reaping*:

> *Do not be deceived, God is not mocked; for whatever a man sows, that he will also reap. For he who sows to his flesh will of the flesh reap corruption, but he who sows to the Spirit will of the Spirit reap everlasting life* (Galatians 6:7-8).

You touch a hot stove and you get burned. God's laws and principles were all revealed to show us where the stove was, so to speak, when it came to our spiritual lives. Our choices have spiritual and physical consequences simply because of how God designed things to work in this world. But when we burned our hand on the stove, God was not judging us. We simply experienced the consequences of our poor choice.

Are there consequences that affect cities and nations? Can innocent people be affected by the consequences of other people's poor choices? Absolutely. The thing that should capture our attention and fuel our passion is not that people are experiencing the consequences of their poor choices, but that we can hold out a message of real hope to them that, in Christ, they can be restored and set free from those consequences!

What about natural disasters and sickness, people ask? Once again, Jesus brought the answers to those problems. He calmed the storms and healed the sick. When the Church starts to *become* the same kind of answer to the problems around us, you can bet that the question of whether God is good or not will come up less. It will be obvious for all to see.

❧ What would happen if God's people stopped trying to explain problems and started to really believe that God is in a good mood all the time, is holding His arms out to every human person, and has a solution to every human problem?

_____

_____

_____

_____

❧ Has there been a situation in your life that has caused you to struggle over the question of the goodness of God? Have you resolved the issue in your heart? How did this affect your faith in God to bring a solution to your problem, or your commitment to your responsibility to offer hope and help to those around you?

_____

_____

_____

_____

PRAYER

Prayer is the bridge between what should be and what will be. The diligent prayer of a righteous people will ultimately determine the destiny of our children. Therefore it is our responsibility to leave to those yet to be born a world in revival as their inheritance. Hanging in the balance of eternity is the ultimate climax of creation—the kingdoms of the world becoming the Kingdom of our God (Vallotton, 224).

Once again, our prayer life is to be founded on the declaration of the Lord's Prayer:

Your kingdom come. Your will be done on earth as it is in Heaven (Matthew 6:10).

This is the ultimate "bridge" prayer—a bridge between Heaven and earth. But the key to building this bridge is *faith*. Faith is expressed in faithfulness and diligence. Consider:

Then He spoke a parable to them, that men always ought to pray and not lose heart, saying, "There was in a certain city a judge who did not fear God nor regard man. Now there was a widow in that city; and she came to him, saying 'Get justice for me from my adversary.' And he would not for a while; but afterward he said within himself, 'Though I do not fear God nor regard man, yet because this widow troubles me I will avenge her, lest by her continual coming she weary me.'" Then the Lord said, "Hear what the unjust judge said. And shall God not avenge His own elect who cry out day and night to Him, though He bears long with them? I tell you that He will avenge them speedily. Nevertheless, when the Son of Man comes, will He really find faith on the earth?" (Luke 18:1-8)

We don't need to question the justice of our God or His timing in bringing it. What we must do is to "cry out day and night." When the cry of Christ's Body agrees with the prayer of Christ, who "always lives to make intercession" for us, and the cry of the Spirit, who "makes intercession for us with groanings which cannot be uttered...according to the will of God", the resonating sound will bring a breakthrough on the earth like we have never seen (Heb. 7:25; Rom. 8:26-27).

The Church was birthed through such a prayer. We read that the believers who waited in Jerusalem "continued with one accord in prayer and supplication" (Acts 1:14). For ten days, their cries invaded Heaven. And then, Heaven, with the "sound...as of a rushing mighty wind" invaded earth (Acts 2:2). The promise that the Spirit would be poured out on all flesh was fulfilled initially, but not fully. It is still the united cry of Christ the Head and Christ the Body that will birth the will of God on earth as it is in Heaven.

❧ Have you experienced praying from Heaven to earth, where God shows you what He wants to do and you cry out in agreement with Him? If so, what was the result of your prayer? Does the knowledge that you're praying in agreement with God help to fuel your faith and persistence in prayer?

_____

_____

_____

_____

❧ Have you spent much time considering the fact that when Christ teaches us to pray, He is teaching us to join Him in what He's doing? What about the fact that Christ and the Spirit are continually praying for you? How might the awareness of those things help to direct and encourage your prayer life?

_____

_____

_____

_____

CONCLUSION

Thank God today for His awesome mercy in your life and ask Him to lead you in showing that mercy to the world around you. Purpose in your heart to take the posture of royalty, where your focus is not diagnosing the world's problems, but bringing the solutions to it. Pray and don't give up!

ENDNOTE

1. C.S. Lewis, *Mere Christianity* (New York, NY: Harper Collins, 1972), 64-65.

RECOMMENDED READING

A Life of Miracles by Bill Johnson

Basic Training for the Prophetic Ministry by Kris Vallotton

Basic Training for the Supernatural Ways of Royalty by Kris Vallotton

Developing a Supernatural Lifestyle by Kris Vallotton

Dreaming With God by Bill Johnson

Face to Face by Bill Johnson

Here Comes Heaven by Bill Johnson

Purity by Kris Vallotton

Strengthen Yourself in the Lord by Bill Johnson

The Supernatural Power of a Transformed Mind by Bill Johnson

The Supernatural Ways of Royalty by Bill Johnson and Kris Vallotton

The Ultimate Treasure Hunt by Kevin Dedmon

When Heaven Invades Earth by Bill Johnson

FOR MORE INFORMATION:

Kris Vallotton
Bethel Church
933 College View Drive
Redding, CA 96003

www.kvministries.com

Additional copies of this book and other book titles from DESTINY IMAGE are available at your local bookstore.

Call toll-free: 1-800-722-6774.

Send a request for a catalog to:

Destiny Image® Publishers, Inc.
P.O. Box 310
Shippensburg, PA 17257-0310

"Speaking to the Purposes of God for This Generation and for the Generations to Come."

For a complete list of our titles, visit us at www.destinyimage.com.